Sisters and Brothers/Daughters and Sons:
Meeting the Needs of Old Parents

Sisters and Brothers/Daughters and Sons:
Meeting the Needs of Old Parents

Sarah H. Matthews, Ph.D.

Unlimited Publishing
Bloomington, Indiana

Distributing Publisher:
Unlimited Publishing, LLC
Bloomington, Indiana

http://www.unlimitedpublishing.com

Contributing Publisher:
Sarah H. Matthews, Ph.D.

Front cover photo by William Morrison; used with permission.
Back cover photo by Pamela Scrutton; used with permission.
Cover design by Pamela Scrutton; used with permission.
Book design by Charles King. Copyright © 2002 by Unlimited Publishing LLC. This book was typeset with Adobe® InDesign®, using the Minion®, Myriad®, and Adobe Jensen® typefaces. This book makes use of one or more typefaces specifically licensed by and customized for the exclusive use of Unlimited Publishing LLC.

Unlimited Publishing LLC provides worldwide book design, printing, marketing and distribution services for professional writers and small to mid-size presses, serving as distributing publisher. Sole responsibility for the content of each work rests with the author(s) and/or contributing publisher(s). The opinions expressed herein may not be interpreted in any way as representing those of Unlimited Publishing, nor any of its affiliates.

First edition.

Copies of this book and others
are available to order online at:

http://www.unlimitedpublishing.com/authors

ISBN 1-58832-067-7

Unlimited Publishing
Bloomington, Indiana

To my father and the memory of my mother,
Ralph and Florence Matthews,

and to my sister, Anne

CONTENTS

PREFACE

THIS BOOK REPORTS the results of an in-depth study of the ways in which siblings in 149 families met the needs of their old parents. The intended audience for the book is scholars and their students in family and gerontology courses, as well as middle-aged children and old parents. The book is written with as little jargon as possible with the hope that it will appeal to students and to those for whom issues related to membership in older families are salient.

Two unusual aspects of the research design made the findings reported here more positive than much of the available literature. First, gerontological and family research focuses disproportionately on adult children who are "primary caregivers." They are often depicted as "burdened" with old parents who require an extraordinary amount of care and cannot participate rationally in its provision because they have Alzheimer's disease. That the findings from these studies apply only to those dealing with demented parents often is ignored. Many parents require assistance in their daily lives, although there is a considerable range, but only some of them require custodial care. By including a full range of older parents in this study, a very different picture of older family life emerged.

Second, "stress" and "burden" are the principal outcome variables in much of the research literature. Adult children often are forced to describe their experience in these terms. Respondents for this study told the interviewers how they and their siblings divided responsibility to meet their parents' needs. Most did not characterize this family labor as burdensome but, instead, saw it as an extension of normal family interaction. These findings, which are much more positive than those in the traditional parent-care literature, may alleviate some of the fears about growing old that both adult children and old parents may have.

The book's contribution to the research literature on family and aging studies lies in its focus on siblings. This research project considered families to be networks whose members take one another into account to accomplish the family labor of meeting the needs of old parents. The data support the argument that the structure of the network — including size and gender composition of sibling groups, and the characteristics of family members relative to one another — affects who does what and whether the division of labor is seen as fair. The case is made that conceptualizing families as relationships rather than roles will lead to better understanding of life in older families.

Many people contributed to this book in various ways. Most obvious are the co-authors of journal articles (see bibliography) on which the book draws. They include, in alphabetical order, Margaret Adamek, Paula J. Delaney, Jenifer Heidorn, Tena Tarler Rosner, and Janet Werkner. Without their contributions, the book would undoubtedly be a lesser product. The project was funded initially in the mid-1980s by a grant from the National Institute on Aging (AG03484). In 1998, I had the privilege of being a Petersen Visiting Scholar in Gerontology and Family Studies in the Department of Human Development and Family Sciences at Oregon State University. My appreciation for the opportunity to focus exclusively on the manuscript for those eleven weeks cannot be overstated. Without that generous support the book would not have been written. To the 298 respondents who were willing to complete questionnaires and explain how they, their siblings, and their elderly parents interacted as an older family, I owe an immeasurable debt of gratitude. I hope that I have done justice to their experiences in the pages that follow. Last, to Jetse Sprey, who has listened to and discussed *ad nauseum* the ideas in this book without ever saying, "Enough!", I owe more than words can say.

Chapter One

Studying Relationships among Members of Older Families

THE LONGEST FAMILY RELATIONSHIPS are likely to be those among brothers and sisters. Responsibilities associated with being a member of the original family do not simply end when siblings reach adulthood. Even though adult siblings and their parents rarely continue to share a household, adults continue to be "children" to their parents and brothers or sisters to their siblings. As adult siblings' networks expand to include partners, in-laws, children, and grandchildren, their ties to original kin may seem eclipsed by this network of new relationships. Most siblings and parents, however, continue to play a role in one another's lives. They typically interact routinely and expect to be able to depend on one another in times of need. When parents become old, siblings' ties to original family members often become more apparent because their elderly parents require a different kind of attention.

Although there is a growing literature on the division of family labor between husbands and wives and fathers and mothers, there is very little that focuses on the ways in which the family labor of meeting parents' needs is divided among siblings.[1] What does it mean to adult siblings to be members of older families? What kinds of things do adult children do for their parents and, more importantly, how do they decide who should do what? How are they involved with one another and with their parents in this stage of family life? This book addresses these questions through analysis of the ways siblings in 149 older families divided the family labor of meeting their older parents' needs. In some families the decisions about who should do what were easy; in others' more difficult. Level of difficulty was related to a number of factors, not the least of which was the size and gender composition of the sibling group.

Unlike much of the research literature on ties between adult children and older parents, this book describes older *families*. The research was designed to explore not only family roles but also family relationships. Adult children were asked to tell about their parents' current situation and their own response and that of their siblings to it. They supplied factual information, such as how far family members lived from one another and how often they saw one another. They answered hypothetical questions, such as "What would happen if your mother fell and was unable to get to a telephone?" Most importantly, however, they were asked to tell in their own words how their parents' needs were defined and met in their family. This meant that they talked not only about themselves and their parents but also about their brothers and sisters, spouses and in-laws, as well as others who were not members of their immediate families.

Too often, studies of families focus on the individual. Respondents who occupy particular gender/lineage positions such as daughter, son, mother, or father are asked to answer questions about their "role." Much of the current knowledge about intergenerational relationships in older families, for example, comes from research on adult children, usually daughters, who are designated as the primary caregivers to frail parents, typically their mothers.[2] This lifts the daughter and her mother out of the context of their family and creates an artificial picture. Families can be broken into pairs or dyads, but it is important to remember that such dyad members usually are part of a larger system in which the other members affect their interaction.

Other researchers choose one adult child to represent a generation.[3] This not only equates adult children who have no siblings with those who do, but it also ignores the effects of relationships between or among siblings in families. In addition, siblings in a family implicitly are cast as interchangeable.

Both of these approaches to studying older families limit respondents to the role of adult child and remove from consideration the other family ties which they take into account as they go about the business of meeting their parents' needs.

In Western societies persons think of themselves as autonomous beings when, in fact, they are products of their interactions with others. Humans are social animals who could not survive without others of their kind. Their actions are not those of isolated individuals but are influenced by others and, in turn, influence those around them. In the social sciences, as well as in everyday language, a vocabulary that adequately captures this interdependence has yet to be developed.[4] The term "filial responsibility," for example, is often used to conceptualize what adult children do for their old parents.[5] The term "filial" means "son-like" or "daughterly" and, as such, directs attention to the parent-child pair rather than to ties among all family members. Some sons and daughters are also brothers and sisters, and those ties affect decisions about how a specific child is "filially responsible." For example, two sons, one with a sister and one with a brother, are likely to interpret filial responsibility differently. Another common term, "role reversal," was coined to capture the situation in which the parent becomes dependent on the child.[6] Again, lost in this image of older family ties is the fact that this "new" dyad often is embedded in a family in which the parent has more than one child and the adult child is also a sibling. Whether all siblings view their tie to the parent as "reversed" is likely to affect decision making about a parent's treatment within a family. The available vocabulary for representing ties among older family members, then, breaks families into intergenerational pairs. The effects that family members have on one another are ignored.

That individuals and intergenerational pairs, rather than whole families, are the focus of research is not surprising. There is no concise way in the English language to distinguish between someone who has a brother and someone who has a sister. Furthermore, knowing that someone is a brother or sister provides no information about the number of others to whom the person is related in this way. The available kinship terms "brother" and "sister" gloss over these issues just as the kinship terms "mother" and "father" provide no information about the number and gender of a parent's offspring.

Families are groups in which interdependence is quintessential. Cultural rules, both formal and informal, link very specific people together into groups in which membership is involuntary. Individuals may neglect familial obligations, but they cannot wish away their family membership. Consequently, family members are entangled in the lives of a web of specific others whose actions affect their own.

Adult children and their parents do not exist simply as individuals but as family members. Gender and lineage positions are important factors in how members participate, but what each member contributes to the family is a function to some degree of what others are contributing. To study families is to focus on reciprocity and interdependence and on the ways members take one another into account when deciding how to act.

The interview guide for this study, then, was constructed on the premise that all adult children in a family are implicated in meeting the needs of old parents, regardless of how and even whether they participate. Throughout the interviews, adult-child respondents were reminded continuously that they were members of a family group and asked to speak not simply as adult children but also as siblings. They were asked to explain what each sibling (including themselves) did and why; also why others (including themselves) did nothing, less or different things.

The interview guide framed how adult children would approach the topic, as is the case in all research that relies on some sort of questionnaire. Had they been asked to answer questions only about themselves, they would have responded differently. In this study, a "vocabulary of relationships" was imposed. When considering their parents, did they view themselves only as daughters or sons, or did they simultaneously think of themselves as sisters and brothers? These questions rarely are raised in research on families, because respondents are asked only about themselves. Evidence that siblings take one another into account, however, is found in research on primary caregivers to parents who require a great deal of care. These caregivers often are reported to complain, sometimes bitterly, that their siblings are not more helpful.[7]

FAMILY SIZE/FAMILY COMPLEXITY

The number of family members is important to consider when the focus is on relationships rather than roles. Obviously, the division of family labor is likely to be different in a family comprising two siblings than in a group of six. Whether both parents are alive also is likely to affect what siblings do for their parents. The smallest and least complex older family eligible for this study consists of three people: an old parent and two unmarried adult children. Ties among the three family members are not independent of one another; each person in the triad is linked both directly and indirectly to each of the others. The tie between any two of the members affects their ties with the other member. Two sisters who agree that their mother is a witch, for example, make it difficult for their mother to cultivate either daughter's affection.

Complexity of a family is a function of the number of possible relationships. It increases exponentially with size. If a family that includes one parent and two unmarried offspring increases in size *either* because both parents are living *or* there is a third unmarried sibling, the number of possible pairs among the four members increases to six and triads are possible as well. Coalitions beyond two-against-one become an option. If the other parent *and* a third sibling are added, the number of pairs among the five family members increases to ten. The principle that dyadic ties within a family are not independent of one another holds in larger families as well.

When siblings are married, the structure of a family is even more complex. Each married adult child links a spouse to the other family members. How these in-laws get along not only with members of their spouse's original family but also with one another becomes an issue. If the respective husbands of two sisters do not like one another, for example, the way in which the two sisters cooperate to meet their parents' needs and how their husbands are involved are affected.

Families do not have to be very large to become complex. This is one of the reasons that social scientists prefer to focus on family roles rather than on family relationships. Even a small family has a complex structure. Nevertheless, family members act within and re-create those structures, affected in some ways that are obvious and in others that are not. One of the goals of sociologists who study families is to make the effects of these structures visible. Ignoring structure because there is no simple vocabulary that facilitates discussion produces unrealistic images of families. By putting family structure at the heart of this book, one goal is to encourage those who study families to go beyond roles and focus on relationships among family members.

MEETING PARENTS' NEEDS

AS FAMILY LABOR

Most of what is known about the division of family labor comes from research on how housework and childcare are divided between husbands and wives.[8] Although not strictly analogous, what adult children do with and for their parents also can be viewed as family labor. Siblings, like wives and husbands, must negotiate a division of labor and perform tasks to accomplish this family responsibility.

There are some obvious differences between being a partner in a marriage and being a sibling. Marriage is a voluntary relationship that can end when either person decides it is over. Siblings, however, cannot divorce, although they, like spouses, may be guilty of desertion and dereliction of duty. Second, a legal marriage comprises two people of different genders. Differences in partners' participation are usually explained by gender. For some sibling groups this explanation is not available. A two-member sibling group may comprise a brother and a sister, but a pair of brothers or a pair of sisters also is possible. In addition, sibling groups can include more than two members. All may be the same gender, one gender may outnumber the other, or there may be an equal number of brothers and sisters. Furthermore, same-gender siblings are unlikely to be identical. There may be many differences between or among them, at least some of which will be significant with respect to who is expected to do what with and for their old parents. For example, fifty families in this study included at least two sisters. In all of these sibling groups one of the interviewed sisters was employed and the other not employed. This difference, however, often was not the only one between the two sisters, and they referred to other differences such as marital status and geographic proximity to explain unequal and specific contributions.

Within these 149 sibling groups, then, evaluation of each member's contributions relative to the others was based, at least to some degree, on comparing siblings' circumstances. In describing who did what with and for parents, their relative standings were important not only for actual behavior but also for what siblings expected of one another. How did they explain and justify unequal and different kinds of contributions? Continuing to use the example of difference in sisters' employment status, did nonemployed sisters do more for parents than employed sisters did? If so, did both sisters see this as fair?

Two Caveats

Two issues that often are included in discussions of older families are not addressed in this book but simply taken as given. First, beginning with empirical research in the early 1960s, the myth of the "isolated nuclear family" was dispelled — at least among scholars[9] — and replaced with the idea of the "modified extended family."[10] It is now well documented that family ties continue to be important both to parents and children after children reach adulthood and that a great deal of exchange, both instrumental and sentimental, takes place among family members.[11] Also well documented is that the bulk of assistance received by elderly parents, particularly if they are widowed, is provided by their adult children. Whether motivated by obligation or love, adult children in most families attend to the needs of their old parents in some fashion. Families vary with respect to level of solidarity, but, on the whole, family members look out for one another. Parents who are abused and abandoned do come to the attention of the public and become clients of social service agencies, but it is important to remember that they are atypical.[12]

John Mogey argues that between generations "amity operates in families:"

> Goods and services, money and love, flow from those who control these resources to those who have need of them. Those responding to the implicit demands of significant others [do so] not to commands from superiors, nor as a result of bargains that are negotiated between status equals. . . . This self-regulating behavior is continuous between members of different generations and remains an important and essential form of social behavior in all modern societies.[13]

Matilda White Riley describes families as a "matrix of latent relationships."[14] Although most research has focused
exclusively on an intergenerational tie rather than on ties
among all family members, there is evidence that interaction
between brothers and sisters also continues and that they
provide assistance to one another as needed.[15] That "amity"
is a part of sibling relationships may be less obvious simply
because, in adulthood, siblings' networks expand to include
spouses, children, and in-laws who, in times of need, often are more obvious sources of support than brothers and
sisters. Sibling ties of ever-single adults, whose own family
networks do not expand in adulthood, are less "latent."[16] In
this book, then, it is simply taken for granted that family ties
endure and that they are consequential throughout life.

The second issue relegated to the background is the effect, both real and projected, of social and demographic
change. In the current gerontological research literature, it
is difficult to find reports that do not make some reference
to the fact that there has been an increase in longevity, a
decline in fertility, and an increase in women's labor-force
participation. These three long-term societal changes obviously affect relationships among members of older families.
Increased longevity means that more parent-child relationships endure into the parents' very old age and the children's
middle or even old age, while a small number of children
in a generation translates to fewer potential caregivers.
Participation in the labor force makes women's lives less
flexible; paid work may compete with family work. Much
research on older families is designed to study or, perhaps
more accurately, is justified by concern about the impact of
these demographic and social changes.[17] It is almost as if the
issues raised would be unimportant if social arrangements
were static. The premise in this book is that understanding how members of older families meet the needs of old

parents is important to know *independent* of demographic and social change. The significance of change is difficult to gauge without adequate appreciation of how actual families are affected by more obdurate features such as their size and gender composition.

Families can have a limited number of gender compositions and sizes. Although the distribution of actual families into various combinations changes through time, there is no reason to assume that formal structural properties will have radically different effects when they are more or less common. Even expectations based on gender, while far from fixed, are unlikely to change dramatically. Research on the division of household labor and childcare indicates that changes in beliefs about "gender-appropriate" behavior have "stalled," to use Arlie Hochschild's term.[18] Historical research also indicates that beliefs about what is appropriate for each gender with respect to family labor are deeply embedded in the culture.[19] The focus of this book, then, is not on what may happen in the future or how the present is different from the past but on how, within different structures, actual family members accomplish meeting the needs of elderly parents. The ways various structural properties affect the ease with which siblings meet their parents' needs provide valuable information about the likely consequences of specific demographic and other societal changes.

CHOOSING OLDER FAMILIES

The 298 adult children who participated in this study met three criteria that, together, define older families in this book. These criteria, what each was intended to accomplish, and how they limit the families to whom these findings are applicable, are outlined below.

Age of Parents

The adult children had at least one parent over the age of 75 who was not residing in a nursing home. This criterion was intended to insure that the families were, indeed, "older." There is no agreement on the chronological age at which someone becomes old. Bernice Neugarten set 75 as the age for distinguishing between the "young-old" and the "old-old."[20] John Logan and Glenna Spitze found that only after age 80 do a majority of people define themselves as old rather than middle aged or young.[21] Somewhat arbitrarily then, 75 was chosen as an age when health problems and frailty, even if they were not current problems, would likely be anticipated, and when adult children would be aware that their parents' remaining years were numbered.

Choosing age, rather than health status of parents, also meant that the full variety of situations that older families experience would be included. Many studies begin with a "dependent" parent, defined as someone who requires or receives assistance to accomplish one or more of a set of specified tasks.[22] In other studies adult children who identify themselves as "caregivers" to a parent volunteer to participate. Both often focus on adult children whose parents are victims of Alzheimer's disease. Findings from these studies have increased understanding of how adult children's lives are affected by meeting the needs particularly of mentally impaired parents. Unclear is the degree to which these findings apply to less extreme situations — which are more typical of life in older families, even when parents are very old.

Marital status of the parent also was left unspecified. Families that include widowed parents, especially widowed mothers, are disproportionately represented in the research literature. Adult children are unlikely to be designated as "primary caregivers" to a parent as long as both parents are alive, because that role is reserved for the less frail parent. Including families in which only the mother, only the father, or both parents were living provided a fuller range of actual situations with which adult children contend.

Gender Composition of Sibling Group

The second criterion was the number of sisters or daughters in the family. Initially, the research focused on families in which there were at least two sisters, specifying further that one sister be employed, the other not. This latter requirement was included in order to address the question: "Compared to her employed sister, does an unemployed sister assume more responsibility for their parents?" Subsequently added were families in which there was only one sister, as well as those in which there were only brothers. By selecting older families on the basis of the gender composition of the sibling group, this study could examine the effects of different combinations of the two genders. Furthermore, sons are much less likely to be included in research on older families. Because parent care is assumed to be "women's work," many researchers have focused exclusively on daughters, with the result that information about brothers is largely secondhand, provided by sisters who often portray their brothers as unwilling to help. In this study, however, at least one brother in two-thirds of the families spoke for himself.

Pairs of Siblings

The third criterion was that two siblings in a family agree to be interviewed. Rather than relying on one member of the adult-child generation to tell about the family, this study expected two siblings to participate. Jessie Bernard was one of the first family scholars to point out the error of assuming that one spouse could speak for the other.[23] She argued that there was "her" marriage and "his" marriage: members of the pair experienced the relationship differently. Regardless of the group under consideration, each person is likely to have a different perspective. This point undoubtedly applies to research on older families. Interviewing two siblings made it possible to compare two versions of the way parents' needs were met. Would the description provided by the adult child who might have been the spokesperson for the family as the "primary caregiver" be corroborated by a sibling? Or would two siblings portray the situation in different ways?

Limitations of the Selection Criteria

Although these criteria accomplished the intended goals — variety of older family situations, families that included sibling groups with specific gender compositions, and two perspectives on how parents' needs were met — the ways in which they limit the findings are important to recognize. First, families in which both parents died before either reached the age of 75 were not included. Adult children in such families coped with their parents' deaths and the time preceding them *on average* at younger ages than those tapped for this research.[24] Sibling relationships may be affected by the age at which children are orphaned. Research conducted by Young and Willmott in the 1950s on English working-class families revealed the importance of "mum." She continued to be a focal point in her children's lives. They kept in touch with one another through her. Her death atomized the family, as each of her daughters became the "mum" to her own children and grandchildren.[25] When adult children are orphaned earlier in their lives because parents die in their sixties or early seventies — *as many do* — the significance of sibling ties, depending on the circumstances, may diminish or become more important. The findings about sibling relationships reported here are only about siblings with living parents. Finally, information about how only children and sole-surviving children meet filial responsibilities cannot be found in this book.

The requirement that a pair of siblings agree to participate introduced another potential bias: older families whose members did not speak to one another were not included. Those who were speaking but whose words were acrimonious may also be poorly represented. Not all of the siblings who did participate were amicable or had only positive things to say about one another. Nevertheless, these pairs of siblings probably are skewed toward the higher end of a continuum of family solidarity.

RESEARCH DESIGN

This research project is qualitative. Rather than asking the siblings to respond only to fixed-choice questions, they also were treated as "informants," experts on their family who could tell the researchers what was important about the experience of having old parents. Although the written questionnaire included fixed-choice questions, as did the face-to-face interview, the information gathered in this way was intended primarily to provide the context for interpreting each informant's description of what went on in his or her family. Sampling was not intended to be representative of a known population but to include families with specific structural characteristics. Some issues are best understood when their incidence and prevalence are known. The pioneering work of Ethel Shanas is a case in point.[26] Understanding how actual families perform the family labor of meeting parents' needs, however, seems better suited to conceptual sampling[27] that leads to an understanding of process and interdependence. The families in this study, then, were recruited in order to gauge the effects of various family structures on the way sisters and brothers meet their parents' needs. They are not a representative sample.

Recruiting Siblings

Recruiting pairs of siblings for the study required considerable ingenuity. Adult children were asked to participate in research on older families with specific gender compositions and parents aged 75 or over. The term "caregiving" was avoided intentionally. The initial families included two sisters — one employed, one not employed. Advertisements were placed in local campus and community newspapers. Various community groups and agencies that had women as participants or clients — excluding caregiver-support groups — were contacted and asked if recruitment fliers could be posted. Occasionally, the person contacted in one of these groups volunteered to participate when she saw that she met the criteria. Usually, the first sister to make contact indicated that she already had spoken with her sister or that she would. Sisters with more than one sister, then, chose the other one who would participate.

Subsequently, lone-sister families (those comprising only one sister and one or more brothers) and brothers-only families (those with at least two brothers and no sisters) were recruited, initially using the same tactics. In lone-sister families, sisters called and volunteered a brother, whom they usually preferred to contact themselves. Again, if a sister had more than one brother, she chose one to participate. Brothers-only families were not forthcoming. Apparently, men did not see themselves as appropriate candidates for research on older families.[28] Almost all of the men in brothers-only families, therefore, were recruited through their parents. A colleague who recently had interviewed community-dwelling elders over the age of 85 had included a question about the gender of their children. Parents in her study who had two or more sons were identified and asked for permission to contact their children. Some of the sister-brother pairs were recruited this way as well.[29] In addition, a registry of elders who had volunteered to participate in research on a university campus was tapped. Calls were made to find out whether their families met the criteria; if they did, parents were asked for permission to contact their children. They were also asked if they knew anyone whose family might qualify and, if they did, for permission to call them. The elders typically were very helpful, and very few of the sons who were contacted said "no" to the request to participate in the study. Gradually, 49 of the 50 brothers-only families originally targeted were recruited. Relying on this registry probably accounts for the somewhat higher social class of the brothers-only families.

Research Instruments and Data Collection

The underlying supposition of the project — that by virtue of membership all adult children in an older family are, at the very least, implicated in meeting the needs of their old parents — had important implications for data collection. Information about the entire family was required, rather than only about one old parent and the adult child designated as the primary caregiver or spokesperson for his or her generation. When combined, characteristics of family members describe structural features of families that set parameters around available options — for example, size, gender composition, geographical dispersion, and members' relative marital, parental, and health statuses.

Once a pair of siblings had volunteered to participate, one was quizzed to determine how many parents, brothers, and sisters were in the family so that a questionnaire that included a set of questions about each family member could be compiled and mailed to each respondent. Information obtained about each adult child and each parent included, for example, place of residence and distance from each family member, marital status and presence of in-laws, number and ages of children and grandchildren, composition of current household, educational attainment, type of job, number of hours worked each week, and health status. In addition to the old parents and adult children, information about extended family members who were linked to the family through its original members — spouses, children, in-laws, and siblings of the old parents — was collected.

If the adult child lived within driving distance of Cleveland, an interviewer called approximately a week after the questionnaire was mailed to make an appointment for a face-to-face interview. Most of the interviews took place in respondents' homes. The interviewer glanced through the questionnaire to insure that it had been completed and to get some idea about family composition, then conducted a face-to-face interview. Siblings who lived too far away to be interviewed in person returned their questionnaires by mail. When the completed questionnaire arrived, it was given to an interviewer who then set up a time to talk with the sibling over the telephone. Prior to the interview, the

interviewer looked over the questionnaire to become familiar enough with the family to minimize the effects of not
having face-to-face interaction.

Over the course of data collection, ten women, in addition to the author, conducted interviews; they ranged in age
from late 20s to early 60s. Each member of the sibling pair
was assigned to a different interviewer so that each heard
only one sibling's version of how parents' needs were met.
Each sibling was paid twenty dollars for participating in
the study.

During the interviews "respondents" became "informants;" each sibling was treated as the expert and assumed
to have a story to tell that the interviewer was committed
to hear and comprehend. The interviewer's goal was to see
the family through the sibling's eyes. The interview guide
and the order of the questions were designed to allow siblings to tell what was going on in their family with respect
to their old parent(s) and one another. The first question
asked the informant to describe the situation of her or his
parent(s). Subsequent questions asked who did what and
why. Questions about parents' networks beyond immediate
family members also were included. The interviewers were
instructed to treat the interview as a guided conversation,
that is, to let the informants relate their experiences in the
order they preferred. Nevertheless, each question on the
interview guide was asked in order, even if the topic had
been discussed previously. Interviewers wrote what the informants said as near to verbatim as possible.

As a qualitative study, the design has a drawback that is
important to note: the interviews were not tape-recorded.
This decision has implications for the interpretation of the
data. In looking for patterns during analysis, it was important to remember to attend to *what* was said rather than *how*
it was said. More subtle distinctions and interpretations

would have been possible had transcriptions of the interviews been available. Another limitation that stems from not recording the interviews is that the interview guide was not modified as data collection progressed, nor tailored to the informant. Rather, the same questions were posed to each informant. As noted above, the interviewers were trained to let the informants "talk themselves out" before asking another question; however, all of the questions were asked, thereby making the interaction more structured than is ideal in a qualitative interview.

The decision not to tape the interviews made it feasible to include a larger number of families than would have been the case had time and money been used for transcribing tapes. The written questionnaire provided a great deal of contextual information and set the stage for the guided conversation. In their own minds, informants already had laid the groundwork, so that when they began the interview, they were elaborating on what they already had told. For analysis and interpretation, the written questionnaire provided a detailed context within which to interpret their words. In addition, two members' versions of what went on in each family produced a fuller picture.

Data Analysis

To facilitate qualitative analysis, data collected through the open-ended interviews were typed into 149 family files juxtaposing the responses of the two siblings that were triggered by each question (the interview guide is included in Appendix I). Family files were read many times as various ideas for analysis were pursued. For a specific code, the entire interview, rather than only answers to specific questions, was mined. For example, informants were asked "what would happen and who would be most likely to be available to help. . .if your parent fell and was unable to get to a telephone?" All of the siblings' responses to this question were collected in one file. In addition, the entire interview was gleaned for relevant data. If at some other point in the interview, a sibling talked about a parent's having fallen or indicated that he or she was worried about this possibility, this remark was also included in the file. As another example, one code pulled together all references to in-laws — husbands, wives, sisters-in-law, brothers-in-law. The in-law file subsequently was coded into ten new files to sort out significant factors in the way that in-law relationships operated in these families. Analysis entailed moving back and forth between coded segments and the interviews to gauge the validity of an argument as it was developed inductively.[30] All of this coding involved reading and rereading, interpreting and reinterpreting not only the coded segments but also the interviews themselves, a process that brought about "intimate familiarity"[31] if not with the actual families, at least with their recorded words.

CHARACTERISTICS OF THE FAMILIES

The findings reported in this book refer specifically to the experiences of siblings in 149 older families. No claim is made that the families are a sample of a known population. It is important, therefore, to know the general characteristics of the families who provided the data that were analyzed for this book.

The 149 families comprised 403 siblings of whom 176 were sisters and 227 were brothers. Of these, 150 sisters and 148 brothers were interviewed. Eight-two families (55%) comprised only the two siblings who were interviewed, 42 (29%)

comprised three siblings, with the other 25 (16%) comprising four to seven siblings.

The siblings ranged in age from 33 to 78. Seventy-seven per cent were married, with brothers being more likely than sisters to be married. More than half of the siblings had graduated from college. Seventy-one percent were employed at the time of the interview, with more brothers than sisters employed. Three families were black; the others white. Catholics, Jews, Protestants, and those without any religious affiliation participated in the study.

The 204 parents in these 149 families ranged in age from 71 to 97, with a median age of 79. Almost two-thirds were mothers. In approximately half of the families (n = 76) only the mother was living, in 12% (n = 18) only the father. One mother and four fathers were remarried. In the remaining families (37%) both parents were alive, and members of 52 of the 55 parental couples were married to one another. In two of the three cases in which a divorce had occurred, the father was remarried. Most of the parents lived in their own households — alone, if they were widowed (n = 63); together, if they were married (n = 50 [100]). In two cases one spouse was in a nursing home, and the other lived alone. Eleven widowed mothers and four couples shared a household with one of their unmarried children (10 with daughters, 5 with sons). Two widowed mothers lived with a son and his family, and one widowed father with a daughter and son-in-law. One widowed mother lived with her sister, and one shared a household with both a daughter and a son. One couple and eight widowed mothers had live-in helpers, and one widowed father and one widowed mother had moved to the assisted-living section of a retirement community in which they had lived for a number of years.

Respondents rated their parents' health status on a 4-point scale from excellent to poor: 28.5% of the sibling informants agreed that their parents' health was excellent or good; 17.6%, that it was good or fair; and 37.2%, that it was fair or poor. For only 3% of the parents (n = 6), did the sibling respondents rank them differently by more than one level on the scale.

With respect to geographic proximity, for nineteen families (13%), no sibling lived within an hour's drive of the parents. In 41 families (28%), only one sibling lived nearby. In 34 families (23%) two siblings lived nearby, and at least one sibling did not. In 55 (37%) of the families, all of the siblings lived near the parents. A few parents wintered in the Sunbelt; so for part of the year, these percentages were different.

OVERVIEW OF CHAPTERS

The chapters that follow describe how members of these 149 families divided the family labor of meeting parents' needs. They begin with the situations of the old parents themselves. Not coincidentally this is where each interview began — with the question, "Would you tell me about your parents' current situation?" Every parent's situation was different, but most striking was that the level of parents' needs varied so widely. Some parents were self-sufficient, others completely dependent. The second chapter, then, emphasizes that requisite family labor is very much a function of parents' needs.

It is impossible to describe parents' situations without also including information about what siblings did for them. Chapter 3 describes more explicitly the kinds of contributions they made. What were the tasks that constituted family labor? Noteworthy here is that the line between traditional family interaction and "parent care" for some siblings was difficult to draw.

Chapter 4 focuses on the *division* of family labor, in particular on respondents' descriptions of how each sibling was involved in meeting their parents' needs. Siblings were not interchangeable. They differed with respect to such things as employment status and geographic distance from parents. Siblings recognized and took into account these relative differences to justify who was doing what in their family and sometimes to condemn a sibling who was perceived as a slacker. In mixed-gender sibling groups, one of the most important differences was gender. This difference proved to be so important that it warrants its own chapter. Chapter 5, therefore, is devoted to differences between brothers' and sisters' ideas about the best ways to meet their parents' needs.

In Chapter 6, parents once again take center stage. Although adult children were asked to focus on how they shared family labor with their siblings, the fact that their parents were not simply care recipients but active participants in how labor was divided was too conspicuous to ignore. Old parents are routinely reduced to mere care recipients in research on parent care; however, in this study siblings depicted them as much more involved in the division of labor than was initially assumed in the research design.

Chapter 7 focuses specifically on contentious older families, those in which siblings expressed unhappiness about one another's participation in the division of family labor. Although family history and personalities played a role, some family structures were more likely than others to produce a division of labor viewed by some siblings as unsatisfactory. Both size and gender composition of the sibling group affected the ease with which a fair division of labor was negotiated.

In the final chapter, this study's novel contributions to understanding later life families are delineated. Focusing on family relationships rather than on primary caregivers provides new and more realistic insights into life in older families. One of the drawbacks of the current research literature is its almost exclusive focus on caregiving. By using age of parents rather than mental and physical status of parents to select respondents, these data provide a more positive picture of ties among members of older families. The benefit of focusing on families as networks of relationships is also highlighted. In addition, by focusing on sibling groups with different gender compositions, this study yielded a richer understanding of gender differences consistently noted in the research literature. By giving brothers the opportunity to speak for themselves, this book uncovers how men care and why they are rarely credited with caring.

CHAPTER TWO

DEFINING PARENTS' NEEDS

ONE OF THE BLESSINGS of this century is that, on average, people are living longer than at any time in recorded history. One result has been that the lives of parents and children overlap longer because their bonds are not as likely to be interrupted by "untimely" deaths. Rather than seeing this as positive, however, research and media attention often focus on how burdensome old parents are to their adult offspring. In fact, increased public and private pension benefits and guaranteed health insurance in the forms of Medicare and Medicaid have reduced parents' dependency on their children. Today most elderly parents not only meet their own financial and residential needs but also often are in a position to assist adult children and grandchildren. It is well documented that many parents continue to give goods and services to their children for their entire lives. Some may require a great deal of help at the ends of their lives, but even then they usually pay their own way and often leave financial legacies that are significant to their children.[32]

Social scientists have contributed to the negative stereotypes of old parents by focusing almost exclusively on those who need a great deal of care. The anguish associated with Alzheimer's disease has led to a preponderance of research on its ramifications for the elderly and their caregivers. Most old parents, however, do not suffer from dementia or other cognitive impairments that rob them of the ability to participate in family life. According to one comprehensive study of those persons aged 85 or older *not* residing in nursing homes, only 15.7% reported moderate or higher impairment in cognitive functioning.[33] By making caregiving for old parents with Alzheimer's disease the primary focus of research, the experiences of members of the majority of older families have been overlooked. This book describes how sisters and brothers in 149 families met the needs of their parents, only some of whom were very dependent — even though all were at least 74 years of age, some in their 80s or 90s.

In addition to the advanced age of a least one parent, the gender compositions of the sibling groups qualified adult children for this study. They were recruited as members of older families, *not* because their interaction with their parents was defined as caregiving. They used their own words to describe their parents' situations. These selection criteria and the type of data collected distinguish this study from research in which caregiving is the exclusive focus; parents implicated in such studies are presumed to be very needy. Typically, adult-child respondents are limited to indicating the functional health status of their parents, whether they perform any of a set of tasks for them and, if they do, how much time they spend performing such tasks.[34] These variables are used to explain the level of stress, burden, or depression adult-child caregivers currently are experiencing. In the research reported here, informants described a much wider range of activities and concerns, because they had latitude to speak more broadly about their parents' situation.

Extraordinary care is not always needed by a parent before she or he dies; even when it is, it may only be required for brief periods of time. Approximately half of persons aged 75-84 report that they have no "health limitations." Those over 85 are equally divided among those who report no limitations, those who report some limitations, and those who are "unable to carry out everyday activities."[35] The 1982 National Long Term Care Survey found that fewer than 20 percent of the elderly respondents aged 65 or over required help with at least one activity of daily living.[36] The relatively good health of their parents disqualifies many adult children from being respondents for research on parent care. This does not mean, however, that family interaction is unaffected by the personal and physical changes that are the inevitable concomitants of old age.

This chapter presents the various circumstances confronted by the siblings, first for those with parents whose current situations seem to belie their advanced years, followed by those in dire circumstances. Parents who were between the two ends of the continuum — the bulk of the situations — are then described. While a diagnosis of Alzheimer's disease officially marks the beginning of a downward descent in capabilities, many of the changes that old age brings are more amenable to recovery and effective adaptations that preserve self-sufficiency. According to these siblings, when changes had occurred in their parents' lives, measures had been taken to mitigate their effects. Parents recovered or adjusted to living with different abilities and social networks. Both uneasiness and cautious optimism were apparent in the ways in which siblings described their parents' lives in these more ambiguous situations.

CAPABLE PARENTS

At one end of the continuum are capable parents (n = 25)[37] whose adult children spoke of them with pride. A sister said that her 81-year-old father "is probably one of the better examples of old age that you'll be dealing with in your study." A brother explained: "This is not an elderly, fragile person we're talking about. She's very strong, alert, active. She's very much younger than her actual age [of 78]."[38]

A sister described her indomitable 86-year-old mother who, ten years earlier, had faced a loss that very old people are of increased risk of experiencing:

> My mother lost a son about ten years ago. I thought she would never survive it — her only son. My sister and I got her busy. We got her a job twice a week — evenings at the church counting money at bingo games. She loves it. It's been fantastic for her. She's living in an enormous home alone — 70 windowpanes and she washes them herself. Up to three months ago, she did everything herself, even the plastering, but now she has hired a plasterer to do it. She does her own marketing and banking. This year for the first time, she's letting a neighbor cut her grass. She did it herself before this. She still does gardening and weeding. She has no physical problem — never even a headache. I remember her being in bed only one day. She hasn't had a physical examination in 55 years. The only problem is that she's too independent and doesn't want to be accountable to anyone.

A brother described his mother, whose only problem stemmed from another hazard that comes with very old age, outliving friends:

She lives in her own home and maintains it completely herself. She will be 89 and is fortunate to have complete health both mentally and physically. She still drives a car, shovels snow, and travels by herself. The biggest support for us to give her is that her circle of friends has diminished and she needs someone to occupy her time, although she has a fairly active social schedule. She lives about three and a half miles from here. Financially she's in good shape. There are no particular problems. She has somewhat of a problem to walk — not in her house, but walking to a shopping center two miles away. The doctor says there's just hardening of the arteries. In the past couple of years she had two cataract operations, the last one in February of this year, and her independence showed when she informed me she had it done while I was on vacation.

A brother, who lived approximately two hours from his parents, aged 82 and 86, described their lives in the small town in which he had grown up:

My father's hearing is fading slightly. When I talked to him on the phone on Mother's Day, I had to repeat some things. He's okay face-to-face. He walks with a stoop. He was a laborer. He has all his hair. He got false teeth at age 45, and he has glasses. He didn't drink or smoke when I was growing up. He smoked for ten years and then quit. He barely drinks. They take vitamins. They swear they have cleared up all kinds of sinus problems. We think they spend too much on them. He's very active. He has one of the best fossil collections in Ohio, and he found them himself walking the fields. He gives lectures about them at public schools. He still walks the fields, but not as often. He can read better now with his glasses. He enjoys TV, sports, and reading. He goes to church fairly regularly. The only operation I know he had was

in the 1950s for kidney stones. Plus the cataracts. He's
about six feet even. Or was. He's bent over now. Other
than that he's fine. . . All of my mother's sisters are
living, six girls and two boys. She's the oldest. One
of the brothers had an injury and fell. He moved in
with one of the sisters [while he was recovering]. My
mother went to watch him while her sister was away.
She got up to get the phone and fell and broke a bone
in her foot. She got a cast. We called to see how we
could help: "Don't need to. Dad will cook. Dad will
shop." We've gone to do major things like painting.
My brother came in to put shingles on the porch. We
help with major things. We don't like them on ladders. When I called Mother's Day, she was back on
her schedule volunteering at the hospital four times
a week. They have led active lives, and they continue
to do so. She worked part-time when we were all in
school. They both receive very good pensions. They
own a home; it's managed well — the shopping's
done, the housework's done. They live in a small
town and know people. They're involved in church
and the lodge. All of her siblings live within a twenty-
mile radius. There's a lot of familial support, almost
a clannish operation. They look after each other and
each other's kids. My wife and I were the first to move
away. I think it's the family support group in the immediate area that's important for them.

A brother described his father:

He's an amazing person — because of his age. He's
having no problems. He's like a teenager. He's 86 years
old. He'll be 87 years old next month. I'm gonna tell
you what he does, and these things are not embel-
lished. He just returned from ten days in Hawaii. He
went to an Elder Hostel in Volcano National Park.
This trip required tramping through the park. That
attests to his vigor and his health. He was hula dancing on stage as a volunteer. Last September he took a

two-week trip to Alaska. He ice-skates twice a week — Wednesdays and Sundays and sometimes Tuesdays. He takes dancing lessons at least once a week. He has a female companion here and there — going around town. He's a painter, so he takes art lessons at the Art Museum as well as at the senior center. He has season tickets to the Cleveland Ballet and the Playhouse. He has a female companion to go with. He goes to an exercise class. He walks four miles every morning. He goes to the Elder Hostels — he's' going to one in Buffalo next week or next month. I don't know; I can't keep up with him. He travels. Goes to Boston to see my brother. He went to Florida. My brother has a place there. He's atypical, to say the least. He has a car. He drives, so he can do all these things. Since he's been a kid, he's had limited eyesight in one eye. As he gets older the other eye is getting worse. When that goes all these things will probably come to a screeching halt.

Two years earlier, his father would have been included in the "in-between parents" section of this chapter because of his wife's poor physical health:

My mother passed away almost two years ago. She had cancer, a very debilitating illness. She had it seven or eight years. The last two years were particularly difficult. It was extremely confining for him. He really didn't do anything. He went ice-skating and to exercise class, but no painting. He stayed close by. After she died, he had the responsibility lifted. He was able to get out. He's had problems, but not health problems. His health is fine. He just has to watch those skin pre-cancers.

A brother described his 87-year-old mother:

Her health situation is fine. She has a little hearing problem, which doesn't stop her. She delivers meals *for* the meals-on-wheels program once a week. She drives her friends around. Financially, she's comfortable: Not rich, not poor. If something has to be done around the house, she will call one of us and we will fix it or get someone to do it. She lives in her own house. Dad died fifteen years ago. She cooks for herself. I'm not aware of any problems now. Nothing in the past either, that I know about. She takes everything in her stride. She's very active in helping people. She's always doing something for someone. She knitted an afghan for my wife's aunt who is in the hospital. She keeps busy all the time.

His brother's assessment of their mother was similar:

You have to make an appointment to see her, except evenings. She doesn't drive at night. Up until now, she's been doing her own wall papering and painting, but we have to keep telling her to stay off of ladders and chairs. And we have to tell her to stay out of bad neighborhoods. She has no fear. She thinks she can just go like when she was younger. If you asked her how she's feeling, she'd say, "If I was doing any better I don't know what I'd do." She's in better shape than I am. She drinks three glasses of hot — as hot as she can stand — tap water every morning. That keeps her bowels regular and her organs functioning. She eats a balanced meal every day between 2-3 PM and she has a high ball — scotch and soda — before every meal.

Despite their advanced age, these parents were remarkably self-reliant. They were affected primarily by the deaths of others rather than by their own infirmities. Their independence, rather than their dependence, worried the siblings but also, obviously, was a source of pride.

DEPENDENT PARENTS

At the other end of the continuum were 20 parents whose infirmities were so debilitating that they would have been in nursing homes or dead if spouses, children, and paid helpers had not been involved in their care. One sister cared for her 86-year-old mother who, two years earlier, apparently had had a stroke within a month of her husband's death. The mother had lived in California near her son, but he and his wife were in poor health and felt unable to help when the mother's health deteriorated; so the sister brought her mother to live with her. When she arrived, according to the sister, "she was skin and bones, but her ankles were badly swollen. I have a lot of guilt. If I had brought her right away after my father died she wouldn't have had that stroke. When she came here, she didn't get any more sandwich spread or salty crackers. Her ankles went down in two weeks." She described part of her daily routine with her mother:

> About 5:30 AM I go into her room. I'm up at 3:00 AM. Her moaning keeps me up. I dress myself. She gets upset if I go into her room with my nightgown on. I think she wants to see me in my work clothes. I get into her place, get her on the commode. I strip the bed because it's wet all the time. I give her applesauce and two Ritz crackers, the kind with no salt. Then I make her oatmeal. She feeds herself; then I put her back to bed. She's in bed all day. She sits up when she eats, but when she's through eating she wants to lay back down. When she has her bowel movement — I can't lift her and wipe her at the same time — so I came up with my own method to do it. I get two paper towels and put them on the edge of the bed. Then I transfer her from the commode to the bed; then I can lay her down on her side and wipe her. It works — you have to come up with ways to do things.

I do the best I can do. She eats about every two hours. At 9:00 AM she has bologna — that's the only kind of meat she'll eat — a piece of cheese, some raisin bread, and coffee. At noon she'll have pears with creamy cottage cheese — she loves that — and pudding with bananas. I just do the best I can do. Then back to bed again. Then, in-between that time I go down and put her laundry in, the sheets. I have to do the laundry every day. The smell of urine would get all over the house.

This mother would not survive without round-the-clock care. The sister had provided in-home care for other elders, giving her the requisite skills; but she said, "It's a lot different taking care of your own mother than it is a stranger."

In a similar case, a brother who had always lived with his parents cared for his 89-year-old father who had suffered a massive stroke fourteen years earlier. To the interviewer's question, "What is he able to do for himself?" he replied:

Zero. He's in bed now. When he goes in the wheel-chair, I put him there. I feed him through a tube in his stomach. I wash him. I irrigate him. Would you like to meet him? I'll show you what good care can do.

His sister described the care arrangement:

My father is totally handicapped, bedridden. You have to do everything for him — feed him, bathe him, get him in and out of bed. He had a colostomy, which helps because we have control over the bags. He has a urine bag as well, and he has a tube in his stomach. You have to feed him that way. He can't eat through his mouth — part of his tongue and throat are paralyzed, so he can't swallow. My brother lives with Mother and Dad. If the weather is good, my brother will take him for a ride or I bring him here for a day. Mother is very arthritic, her hearing is

impaired, and her eyesight is failing. She's going to
have cataract surgery in April. She can hardly walk;
she uses a walker. My brother doesn't work; he lives
there. A nurse comes in two days a week. I go twice
a week and more if I'm needed. The situation is sad,
but my mother has good spirits. She realizes she has
a good family. If she didn't have us, she'd be in a
nursing home with my father.

According to the sister, she and her mother had provided
most of the care for the father for nine years following his
stroke. The brother had taken over five years earlier after
he lost or quit his job.

Another brother lived with his 94-year-old mother who
had short-term memory problems:

Well, she's basically totally dependent upon me. I have
someone come in to give her a bath every Tuesday.
That's the biggest problem. For me it's uncomfortable
for a son to be bathing his mother. I do the cooking,
shopping, paying bills. She leaves everything entirely
to me now. She is able to get around. She used a cane
for a while but lately she hasn't. She uses it outside.
At times, when I call her to dinner, I help her out of
the chair. She's a little unsteady until she gets going.
Healthwise, she has an enlarged heart, rheumatism.
The right knee is the one that's bothering her.

He said that he and his three brothers had had a meeting,
"looking into the future:" "She's on a waiting list now for
a nursing home because I don't know what her situation's
gonna be a month from now, physically and mentally."

Together, two brothers cared for their 79-year-old mother
and their 80-year-old father whose relationship was acrimonious. One brother who lived seven miles from his parents
explained:

My father has never been specifically diagnosed but has had Alzheimer's for the last five years at least. My mother is not sympathetic where he is concerned. He abuses her more because he doesn't control his tongue. It got to the point where she had a stroke. We put them in two homes. My mother went to a private [board and care] home; an aunt was there already. She didn't like it: everybody smoked and they had lots of cats. My father ran away from his home twice. The second time he took a swing at an attendant and the man said, "Get him out of here." So we moved my parents home but put them in separate bedrooms. My younger brother lives with them. He worked part-time but now he works full-time. My father seems to give my mother more respect when my younger brother is around. My brother writes notes to remind them to do things. He does the shopping and sees that they are doctored. My mother is mobile. She still polkas. Her vision is impaired in one eye. My father is afraid to go out, except occasionally he'll just take off and we have to call the police. Last time Mother called me when he put on his coat. I went over and took him for three short walks, which wore him out, so he calmed down.

The brother who lived with his parents portrayed them similarly:

Two years ago my mother had a mild stroke, and that's why I'm back living here in my parents' home. Her right side is affected. My dad has Alzheimer's. He's lost his vocabulary. He reads all the time but can't remember. This is their home, and I live with them. My mother's vision is bad. She's a diabetic and vision is her only problem. Dad can't remember, and it's hard to give him even simple instructions. He can't get to the bathroom fast enough. He has to be watched almost constantly. Doors have to be locked because he just walks out the door. We have had to call the police. When he leaves the house, he can't find his way back. There were no problems until Mom had her stroke. My brothers and I put them in a boarding home after the stroke, but that didn't work out. They were in two separate homes, and he ran away and the police had to come, but I found him. So I came back to live here, and they both came home.

"Forgetful, moody, sometimes nasty, and selfish — she was always somewhat that way, but it's more so," a sister said of her 78-year-old mother who had recently been diagnosed as having Alzheimer's disease. The closest brother lived approximately an hour from the small town in which their mother resided, the sister approximately two hours away, and another brother four hours from her. The geographically closer brother described his mother's situation and also his own frustration and anguish in trying to deal with it:

> She lives alone in a single-family home in a small town and has lived there all my life. She's unable to perform jobs that have sequential tasks associated with them, such as meal preparation, house maintenance, and finances. Her short-term memory is very poor. By that I mean she cannot remember things said in the same hour that they're said. She's unable to retain or understand a schedule of visits. She does not know that her meals will be prepared for her or that she'll be visited. The significance is that she doesn't anticipate visits. She will cannibalize frozen foods for whatever is in them that's edible. She doesn't realize that this is strange behavior. She has a recent history of a cat problem. Currently she has two cats. Last summer one cat bit a neighbor child. The health department came in, and we were in court. Since then we've taken out about two dozen cats. She's currently under a local court order. She cannot have more than two cats on

the premises. She's very resentful of my brother's, my sister's, and my assumption of responsibility for her. Depending on her mood, she gets angry, yells. We end up having to leave. She's ambulatory — all her physical limbs are fine. Outwardly, she looks okay. She appears to maintain minimal hygiene. If we don't visit her on a regular basis, our experience has been that refuse will build up — just be left lying around. Her medical evaluation stated that she should not be left alone for more than an hour. The stove has been turned off. A microwave was put in to be used by the caregivers in preparing meals. She doesn't even remember why the stove is off — she can't retain an explanation. She does not wander outside the house. Her nocturnal activities are a subject of concern. My sister has spent the night, and there was activity during the night. She does not have a car. She's under a court order not to drive. Her car was transferred to my sister. This court order was initiated when she bumped somebody. She also was operating a vehicle without a license. After she was discharged from the hospital a few months ago, we set up a schedule among the three children plus a local caregiver. Monday, Tuesday, Thursday and Friday, she gets meals-on-wheels at noon and she has a dinner-hour visit by the local caregiver. I visit Wednesday and Sunday. My brother and sister visit alternate Saturdays. . . .She does not like to talk about going to a nursing home. Those two topics, money and where she'll live, create a bad relationship between us. I go to an Alzheimer's support group. That helps. And I have a wonderful wife. Mom resents that I have title to her home, a result of a tax debt seven years ago that she could not satisfy. At the time it was voluntarily done; she was grateful at the time. Over time it became a source of hostility; so I stopped visiting. I resumed my visits last fall. I became concerned because of the cats and the driving. I emptied the house of all her paperwork, unbeknownst to her. I went through it all, organized it. I saw she no longer had any money. She bounced checks in the summer. She spent a $10,000 gift from her sister over 6-7 years. The house was a mess. I began visiting her twice a week and contrived to get her into the hospital. The theme of this whole thing has been deception. I have to lie about what we've done. I explained to her directly about her car being transferred to my sister, about my name being on her checking account, where her cats are. I had to apply for Medicaid in case she has to go into a nursing home, and I had to get her signature. I was direct then, but now when she asks about any of these things, I have to use deception. Otherwise, she just gets so angry and resentful. It does not please me to have to use deception. I feel very sorry for her.

More is said below about the effects of residential proximity of family members and parents' personality characteristics, both factors that exacerbated this situation.

The dependent parents described thus far had cognitive impairments that made it impossible for them to participate rationally in their own care. Other parents who required extraordinary care were mentally alert. A brother described how he and his household members cared for his very infirm 78-year-old mother who lived with them. That his wife was a nurse made possible the decision not to place his mother in a nursing home.

Seven months ago she moved to a retirement center — we thought that would be for a fairly long time. She's had trouble swallowing for a long time. There have been problems following up with doctors — different medications for arthritis and general aches and pains. She was having some breathing problems. One Saturday she took a turn for the worse. We took her to the hospital. They found out she did not have much of a gag reflex — she was getting food in her lungs. She had heart problems while she was in the hospital. They ruled out a lot of things, but they couldn't determine exactly what it was due to, possibly a stroke. She had been in the coronary care unit and had a ventilator. The doctor recommended a tracheotomy, but she opted not to. She does have a tube for feedings. The doctors are surprised she's come along as well as she has. Since she's been here [in his home], her strength has increased. Her calorie intake is better. Her nutritional health is better now than in the last couple of years. We also do breathing treatment three times a day — inhaler, cupping, and clapping on the back. Four of the five of us who live here can do that. She just had cataract surgery on one eye a few weeks ago. My wife tried to counsel her out of it, but it went okay. She's supposed to get her second eye done eventually. They're planning on doing a cookie swallow — take x-rays as she's swallowing — mainly because my mother wants to see if the swallowing is coming back. Once in a while she'll have ice cream. Once she had mashed potatoes and gravy. She coughed some. When she first came out of the hospital she didn't want to live. Cooking and food preparation was her life. It was very discouraging for her. She still goes to Adult Day Care three days a week. She's one of the younger ones. Sometimes it's discouraging to her: she sees how much longer she has to live. Sometimes she goes on outings but has trouble walking. She uses a quad cane. If she goes to the shopping mall she uses a wheelchair or she walks behind the shopping cart.

The parents in these older families required a great deal of care, most supplied or supervised by family members who went to exceptional lengths to insure a parent's survival.

IN-BETWEEN PARENTS

The bulk of the parents included in this study fall between these two ends of the continuum. They were not completely self-sufficient nor did they require intensive supervision or hands-on care. Instead, they were dealing with physical changes (infirmities, diseases, diminished sight and hearing) and changes in social networks (widowhood, loss of friends, changes in residence) that strained their personal resources, required adjustments in life styles, and increased their reliance on others to meet needs and remain secure. Many factors came together to make changes in their lives more or less problematic to them and to their children. Each parent's situation was unique, but running through the data are four factors that in combination affected their independence in ways that the siblings said were significant. These are: discrepancy between parents' levels of need, parent's personality, place of residence, and composition of a parent's immediate social network. The last two factors are difficult to disentangle and, therefore, are discussed together.

Parent Couples

One-third of the families in this study included both a father and a mother. When both parents are alive, the less-infirm one usually is designated as the primary caregiver for research purposes, and their children's contributions rarely are examined. In the 55 families in this study in which both parents were living, siblings were very much involved. Problems arose when one parent was in considerably better health than the other was. The difference made decision making difficult because it affected and was negotiated with two parents rather than one.

Siblings described difficulties that stemmed from discrepancies between parents' abilities. A sister said that she had come to accept that her 77-year-old father was physically disabled but believed that her 77-year-old mother had difficulty accepting it. Her father's health had deteriorated over the past seven years.

> Emotionally my mother is not too happy. She's confined to the house, caring for him. He is ambulatory but has a tendency to fall. On one fall he broke his hip; so she is very cautious with him. She takes him to the doctor, to get his haircut, and shopping; but she must be with him. My dad isn't happy either. He seems to have given up. He gets up, takes his medicine, and goes back to bed. Then he'll get up for lunch; visits a little, then goes back to bed. My mother thinks he's not trying. He acts as though he's had so many problems he doesn't want to try anymore. When my brother or his children visit, he puts on an act and becomes excited and perks up somewhat. My dad's been like this for several years. He's stable in this mode. Each time he's hospitalized, he becomes more confused. We accept him where he's at. There's nothing to do. Mother is frustrated. She thinks if he'd do his exercises, he'd be more mobile.

The sister faced not only her father's decline but also her mother's apparently unrealistic expectations of her father.[39]

A brother described a decision made in the best interest of his 73-year-old mother that left his 75-year-old father in a difficult position. His parents had recently moved from Cleveland, where he and one of his brothers lived, to live with his other brother in another city. At the time of the interview, he was not sure that his father would abide by the decision of the rest of the family:

Mother is very ill with rheumatoid arthritis. She was just released from the hospital after having an implanted hip dislocate for the second time in a year and a half. That caused a lot of mental despair on her part. She can't move without assistance. She's totally crippled. She's now living in Boston with my brother and his family, which is also difficult for my father. He retired ten years ago and has been taking care of her, but he feels that his freedom has been taken away from him due to the fact that Mom has to be taken care of. She can't move, and it's getting increasingly difficult to take care of her. He is just as confined as she is. He is in pretty good shape, but he is physically drained and emotionally, too, because of taking care of her. Financially it's adequate; they are managing. My dad is coming back here. He's supposed to stay here and sell the house and go back to Boston, but he is fighting it. He hasn't totally accepted it. He wants the freedom of being in his own house. The physical change, the relocation, and the progression of the disease are all problems that we and they are facing right now.

One of the reasons cited for the move was that their father would be able to participate in a thriving, ethnic community in Boston. The move was intended to benefit both parents, but the father apparently had some misgivings about whether the decision was right for him, a concern with which his son was sympathetic.

One brother said: "My mother [aged 72] has had over 100 heart attacks. She can spend two months a year in the hospital, and it is increasing. My mother has been bed ridden for about fifteen years." On the other hand, his father, aged 78, was "very healthy and can shoot par golf." The brother credited his father with doing "everything for Mom himself — washes, cooks, bathes, cleans, and handles medications," although his only sister claimed to do much of this. The brother said, "The biggest problem is the care. Dad doesn't want help, and Mom doesn't want to be left alone." The sister described her concerns:

> My father has a hearing aid, but it doesn't seem to help much. We also installed a buzzer close to her bed, but for some reason he doesn't answer the buzzer. He says she only wants a drink of water or some slight thing; so he doesn't answer it right away. Several times it has been an emergency. One time she almost died. He says, "I'm doing the best I can." Those are his famous words. My mother just keeps complaining to us all. We hired a nurse's aid to come in and spend days with her. Each one of us paid for one day. That didn't work out. She was lazy and ineffective.

Negotiating adequate care for their mother was difficult in part because she was also a wife.

In another family, a sister described their parents, who lived in a small town in which neither she nor her sister resided:

> My father [aged 82] doesn't want to talk about going into a nursing home or an apartment connected to a hospital. He gets up and walks out of the room if you talk about that. The minister came to talk about moving into a Methodist home, and father got angry with him, too. I think Mother [aged 79] would go tomorrow if arrangements were all made for her. My mother knows something should be done, but she won't unless my dad would go.

One of the sisters suspected that their father was physically abusing their mother but felt that there was little she could do.

Siblings who had two parents whose needs were different had to respect the integrity of their parents' marriage. Sometimes their concern was that the less capable parent was receiving inadequate care; sometimes, that the more capable parent was jeopardizing his or her well-being to attend to the less capable parent. Identifying a solution that would be optimal for both parents seemed insurmountable.

Personality of Parent

Personality was another factor to which siblings referred in assessing a parent's situation. The "personality disorders" that have received the most attention in the research literature are associated with Alzheimer's disease and other cognitive impairments. These afflictions mean that parents are unable to participate fully in decisions about their own care. Other personality attributes, both positive and negative, were important to the siblings in their assessments of their parents' needs. How each affected siblings' assessments is described in turn.

Two sisters told of their 79-year-old father who had had a stroke sixteen years earlier that left him partially paralyzed on one side. According to one sister: "He kept on going. He didn't fall apart. He didn't miss any work." With the aid of public busses in good weather and their 74-year-old mother in bad weather, he had continued to work as a CPA. The other sister said: "My father refuses to let his health interfere with him. He's been willing to adjust."

A brother listed his 76-year-old mother's numerous operations: "She's had about ten in all, but she has bounded back each time." Her current problems included diabetes, back pain, and loss of eyesight in one eye from a cataract operation "that was not entirely successful;" but "she does her own housework, cooking, and shopping." His 76-year-old father had had a heart bypass operation several years earlier "but is in good health now." He concluded: "Both have handled their problems well. Mother is naturally positive, an outgoing person." Had she not been "naturally positive," the brother undoubtedly would have described her situation differently.

A brother whose 83-year old mother lived in a retirement community attached to the nursing home in which his 89-year-old father lived, said of his mother: "We take care of her problems as they come along. Just take one day at a time. She's lived a sheltered life. Her problems are very easy to discuss. She's not a complex person at all."

A sister described each of her parents, both aged 75, choosing adjectives that indicated that they were not complainers:

> My mother's arthritis is fairly crippling. She uses drops several times a day for glaucoma. She drives and pushes herself. She doesn't let up. She does washing, cooking, cleans house. I only do the ironing. I admire her for it even though I worry about her working as hard as she does. My dad is a go-getter. He keeps busy, does mechanical things around the house. I do see him slowing down a bit. He does snow blowing for our house and for neighbors. He does the shopping. She rarely goes with him. He never did it before, but now that he's retired he enjoys it. He knows bargains, does price comparisons.

A brother explained to an interviewer how his parents, aged 75 and 77, had been able to avoid problems: "Both are optimistic. They seem to recognize what is in their control and what is not and to deal with the former and not waste worry on the latter." Parents' acceptance of what fate had dealt them and a willingness to be positive in the face of adverse circumstances enabled their children to view them positively.

At the other extreme, some parents were portrayed by their children as overwhelmed, bored, or depressed. They did not exhibit a fighting spirit. Their poor choices and complaints pained their children. A brother said:

> My parents [aged 73 and 74] spend most of their life in bed — not in the same bed. They spend most of their days sleeping. They get up at noon, they eat, stay up for a while, go back to sleep, get up around 3:00, stay up at 3:00, have a drink, have dinner, watch the news, a couple of game shows, then go back to sleep. They probably sleep 18 hours a day. It's a sad situation. Dad can do whatever he wants to do. Mom has deteriorating nerves. She never exerts herself to do anything. Deteriorating nerves only deteriorate further if you don't do anything. Dad retired seven or eight years ago. When he worked, it was 17 hours a day. He was an attorney. Mother never had to do anything. She always spent time in bed. Dad never developed any interests; so when he retired he had nothing to do.

His brother said that he had tried to talk to them: "They just go on the way they are. We've tried and my brother's tried. I go over there and I get mad and I say to my dad, 'I can't believe what goes on in this house, or the lack of what goes on in this house.'"

One sister worried because her 78-year-old mother was so unhappy as a widow:

> All of her friends' husbands are still alive. Even though they're not well, they are there. Of course, she bitched like hell when my father was alive and had Alzheimer's; so she complained then, but she's com-

plaining now that he's gone, too. She can't get herself to go out and do something. There's always a reason for her not going out. But then she's always been a homebody and a crazy clean housekeeper — does her cupboards every other week. Her health is excellent. She's bored. She'd love to travel, but she has no one to travel with. I went with her to visit some relatives in Tucson and San Francisco, and it was the first time she'd smiled since Dad died. Her main problem is she is bored, her lack of interests in life other than cleaning her home.

After having lived briefly with her son and daughter-in-law in an in-law suite, a mother moved to a town in which she had lived for many years. The sister who lived a three-hour drive from her reported:

> She lives in a retirement community. It's four floors, and she is in a one-bedroom, assisted-living apartment. She retired at 60 and she is now 90. She's very feeble due to arthritis, which comes and goes. She falls. She's fallen twice this fall. She had shoulder surgery seven or eight years ago, and she can't lift her right arm too well. She's been totally deaf in one ear all her life and now half deaf in the other. Mentally she's great. Her memory is fantastic. She's feeling sorry for herself and adjusting to being away from her family. She calls her fellow residents "inmates." I think she feels neglected by her family, but that is unfounded. She is very busy down there.

For these last parents, even when they were physically capable, their negative attitudes and lack of pragmatism made it difficult for their children to feel positive about doing things with and for them.

Residence and Composition of Social Networks

How change affected parents' abilities to manage their lives also was a function of type of housing, level of integration in a community, and proximity to adult children and other potential helpers. This was apparent in one case, cited above, in which parents had grown old in a small town where they continued to be good citizens and were surrounded by a kinship network that stemmed from the mother's large, original family. Change in these parents' status was accommodated relatively easily.

This was also the case for an 87-year old father who continued to reside in a single-family home with his 85-year-old wife:

> My father has a very comfortable situation. He has a very good second marriage. He remarried about seven years ago. He has the same man tending the house and the same secretary. His wife is a nurse. They have been friends for many years. He is very well situated both financially and healthwise. Fifteen years ago he had a bad automobile accident. He had broken ribs. We were living in Massachusetts at the time and came in to see him. He recuperated thoroughly. Then he had a massive heart attack about twelve years ago. He overcame that and has not had one since. He is hard of hearing. He is not as spry as he used to be, but he will chair a meeting of 150 people and do very well. He has a great sense of humor. He had a business when he was younger, which my two brothers now have, and that increased his worth to a great extent. His mind is very sharp, and last week he drove 850 miles in two days from Maine to Cleveland. My dad is a great man.

Without resources including money and a supportive social network, changes in this father's status would not have boded nearly so well. It is this obvious point that is necessary to keep in mind when assessing the circumstances of these in-between parents.

When parents lived in retirement communities, siblings often reported that they were independent because the setting itself made them self-sufficient. One brother described his 86-year-old father who lived in a retirement community:

> Basically, he's always been a very independent person and still is. He has a hearing problem and a related balance problem in walking. The hearing problem has given him difficulty throughout his life. He's had to fake it a lot. It's getting him into more trouble now. He's still driving. He's not afraid to go anywhere. His world has narrowed quite a bit since my mother died a few years ago. He never did read a lot nor do hobbies or sports. His work was his hobby and his recreation all rolled into one. He lives for his mail, waits for it. He knows what's going on in the world. He reads the paper. He can hold a conversation if he can hear and understand. He's a hypochondriac, but he takes care of himself. He doesn't complain about it, but he's concerned about his health constantly. There are no health problems, except for the aneurysm. That's ongoing. He's independent. Like most people he doesn't like to admit he needs help when he does. The doctor told him several years ago to use a cane for his balance. He just ignores it.

His brother's description was similar, except that he said: "He has a girlfriend, 80 years old, in very good health and has been a good companion to him. She lives just two doors down from him." Their father had numerous physical problems that would be much more problematic for him and the two brothers had he been living in a single-family home. He also was not isolated: the setting provided access to at least one friend.

Apartment complexes that have a high proportion of elderly occupants also were described as significant. A sister, after listing her 76-year-old parents' numerous health problems but emphasizing that they "have a busy social life," said: "They live in an apartment building where they have many friends. There are more older than younger people in the apartment building, but it is not specifically for the elderly."

Loss of a spouse is the most consequential change in a parent's social network. Old parents who lived alone were seen as less secure. A sister said of her 90-year-old mother:

> My father has been dead for four years, and now she's got no one close to watch her. We had round-the-clock help at times in the last two years, when she had the partial mastectomy and the eye operation that resulted in poor vision. She manages her own household, and we help with big things. But she doesn't want anyone around to help. She doesn't manage grocery shopping, but she cooks for herself, dusts, washes her own clothes.

Two infirm parents sharing a household made the proverbial whole bigger than the sum of its parts, even when siblings were concerned about discrepancies in their parents' abilities.

Parents who live in single-family homes in urban and suburban areas were likely to encounter more difficulties than those who lived in congregate settings and small towns. Siblings were more concerned about their everyday welfare. Parents were more likely to be isolated. Their homes had been designed for physically able people, often having at least two floors, yards that needed mowing in the summer and raking in the fall, and driveways that required attention in the winter. These parents often relied more on others to meet their needs, and children were more concerned about their everyday welfare.

Sometimes the homes came with too much acreage to maintain easily. A sister said of her 78-year-old parents:

> Last year my husband and I cut the grass. It's a big lot. It takes two-and-a-half hours every week. I've asked my sister for help. My mother pushed more earlier. She kept going better. She did more outside work. My father can do things, but he's slow. The way they ask — "When you have a chance, please come . . ." — the way they ask, you just want to go. My father never talks about his physical condition to me. My mother will. She'll say, "It hurts," or "I'm tired." For their age, they've done pretty well.

A brother said that his 79-year-old mother was "still living alone in a large house":

> There's a good deal of property that goes with the house. When my dad died twelve years ago, she vowed she would stay there until she died. The place is becoming too much for her to manage. It's the house Dad built. She is getting to the point where she can't do what she needs to. She does worry a lot and keeps a lot to herself. I think it's an attempt not to worry me. She had an injury from an auto accident, in her shoulder. She has angina. She had angioplasty last summer. She just had a breast biopsy. She gets very discouraged healthwise. She has a piece of property in a very desirable location, and she's being pressured to sell it. She still makes her own decisions.

Some parents lived in urban neighborhoods that siblings viewed as unsafe. A brother expressed concern about his 91-year-old mother:

> My mother has lived in public housing for eighteen years. She has been widowed for twenty-seven years. She has an enlarged heart, but her health is pretty good and she's very alert. She has had cataract and knee surgery. We are trying to move her to another public housing building because this area has problems and she no longer feels secure. She no longer goes out herself. Either my sister or I take her out. Her problem is that she is trying to move to another senior citizens building.

Parents who had moved out of long-time homes into more manageable quarters seemed to experiences less serious disruptions associated with social network and physical changes than did parents who still occupied large single-family homes or lived in inhospitable or isolated locations.

Changing residence is a pragmatic way to deal with changing abilities. In fact, many of the parents in these 149 families had recently moved, were in the process of moving, or were thinking about moving. When parents decided to move, the adult children viewed the choice as significant. They worried about whether their parents were making the best decision, and rightly so, as this sister indicated while describing the current situation of her 80-year-old mother:

> Her problem is that she moved only six months ago. The change in apartments, even though it was just across the street and it was her decision, disturbed her greatly. She was so depressed we were thinking of going to a social worker. She refused. She is out of it now, partially. We had an 80th birthday party for her, and it was great and so was she. She has come out of the depression a great deal, but does revert at times.

Her sister also expressed concern about their mother's change in residence:

> When the move was made to this new apartment it was harder for her to make friends. She says it's "couples only" in the new apartment building. But she seems to be adjusting.

One sister described her 85-year-old father's recent move, which was intended to enhance the level of social support he and his wife received:

> My father and stepmother live in a senior citizen high-rise; and my stepmother's daughter, who is 65 or so, lives there also. She's disabled with arthritis. She and my stepmother are close. Father likes high-rise living. He moved to this one to be near his wife's daughter who helps them a great deal with meals. It's a mixed blessing having her there, because she's one other person my stepmother perhaps prefers to him on occasion. He likes this place, though.

A sister indicated that she was afraid that her mother's impending move would make her unhappy because she would be too far from her friends:

> My parents, brother, his wife, and three children are about to move to a newly built home in a suburb that will have an in-law suite for my parents. My mother [aged 73] is apprehensive about moving. She belongs to all her "little groups" where she lives now and is concerned about finding new friends. My father [aged 81] likes the idea. My father has hypertension and can't get around well. And he is getting worse. His life is gardening, and he'll continue to grow his flowers even if he has to crawl to do it. Mother is

involved with many groups and friends and has no health problems. I don't think of my mother as old.

Difference between her parents' abilities is also evident in this sister's concern.

Combining households made it easier for one sister to assist her mother:

> My mother is widowed and is going to be 90 in a couple of weeks. Financially she's well set and has no problems. For 90 her health is pretty good. My brother and my mother lived in a big house, and they decided to move and come here to live. She had a very slight stroke. Her foot was hurt, but she seems okay now. She's slowing down. Up until a month ago, she was washing clothes and I think she will do it again. She uses a wringer machine and won't use my automatic machine. She has had colitis for about fifty years and has been in the hospital four or five times with it over the fifty years. The only problem is her health, which is good, and I take her to the doctor. We go once every two weeks now because of the stroke. She has been weakened by it, but when I talk to her she says she is getting better. I believe that and so does she. She cooked dinner last night.

One brother said that his parents, aged 79 and 83, had moved from a single-family home into an apartment some time ago but now were concerned that they did not live near any of their children:

> My parents live in an apartment. They have been there eleven years. Before that, they lived in their home. My father's heart attack was in April of this year. He's been doing well since then. There are times when he

forgets and repeats things. Since his heart attack it's
a bit worse, but not too bad. My parents are now talking about finding a place, a retirement community,
nearer to one of their three sons. They did look at a
place near my brother when they visited him.

Although health status was an important consideration
in categorizing parents as "in-between," there were other
factors that mitigated health problems. Parent couples sometimes meant that a discrepancy between the abilities of the
mother and father made decision making more difficult. At
the same time, when parents shared a household, siblings
knew that parents were keeping an eye on each other. How
parents faced the vicissitudes of aging also was an important
consideration. Parents with positive attitudes and a fighting
spirit were easier for siblings to deal with than those who
seemed overwhelmed by the changes in their lives. Lastly,
how supportive the environment was, including both residence and social networks, mediated the effects of changes.
Those who lived in single-family homes that challenged their
abilities and who were socially isolated were more likely to
be worrisome to the siblings.

In this chapter the siblings' descriptions of their parents'
situations were presented. Despite the fact that most of these
parents were over 75, some well over 80, siblings described
situations that ranged from self-sufficiency to complete
dependency. Most parents were somewhere in between. It
was not simply functional health status that siblings used to
gauge their parents' needs but the interplay among parents'
abilities, attitudes, and living situations, both physical and
social. The data contained in this chapter include information about what siblings did for their parents. In the following chapter this topic is considered more systematically.

CHAPTER THREE

INTERACTION BETWEEN SIBLINGS AND THEIR OLD PARENTS

THIS CHAPTER DESCRIBES what brothers and sisters did with and for their old parents. This information serves as a backdrop to subsequent chapters in which the division of family labor becomes the focus. Here the types of interaction and the array of services that siblings provided to old parents are described. When siblings viewed their parents as capable, they resisted attempts by interviewers to cast interaction as somehow related to their parents' age or health status. Even when parents' circumstances were more precarious, children did not necessarily view the time they spent with their parents as qualitatively different from what it had been in the past. To understand interaction among older family members, then, it is necessary to take a broader view than "caregiving": providing services is only one of the outcomes of, or reasons behind, siblings interacting with their parents.[40]

Two important factors run through the discussion of what siblings did with and for their parents: gender differences and geographic proximity. Some tasks were more likely to be performed by sisters, other tasks by brothers, although

contact between parents and siblings was not obviously related to gender.[41] Specific services that were associated with
gender are identified using the term "gender appropriate."
Whenever the term is used, it is intentionally placed in quo-
tation marks to indicate that however taken-for-granted
these assumptions are, services are not inherently gendered.
The other important factor underlying what siblings did for
their parents is geographic proximity. Siblings' interactions
with their parents differed depending on how near parents
and siblings lived to one another.[42] In subsequent chapters
gender and geographic proximity are two factors that continue to be important.

The final section of this chapter examines the ways in
which the siblings' spouses were involved in interaction with
their parents-in-law. For those who married into the family, gender and geographic proximity also were significant
factors, but important as well was the degree to which a
spouse embraced or was embraced by the family into which
she or he married.

TRADITIONAL FAMILY INTERACTION

The line between traditional interaction and service-
oriented interaction was sometimes difficult for siblings
to draw. A sister who had very young children said, "My
parents come here to dinner every other week":

> We don't have to provide much for our parents. What
> we do is provide comradeship, and that works both
> ways. When I go shopping with my mother, I need
> her warm body. She needs my companionship. I'm
> dependent on my mother. I need someone to open
> doors for me when I use the stroller. It's a mutual
> support system, not a caregiving one.

Another sister described how she and her sister included their mother in their lives:

> I have both grandmothers here every Sunday. I pick my mother up and take her shopping, but she still drives and goes to church every morning. She shovels her own driveway. She's with my sister on Tuesday and Saturday. We will go out to lunch.

A brother emphasized that his current interaction with his parents was not out of the ordinary:

> They really do 90% of daily activities by themselves. My sister seeks out specialists or new doctors for them. They do their own laundry, cooking, cleaning, and driving around. I take Dad to flea markets on Sundays. We both visit, my sister probably more than I do.

Another brother said: "I talk to Mother on the phone once a week and see her once a week. There is no division of tasks. There are only social things we all do together." As they aged, family members continued to be part of one another's lives. Providing services was not necessarily viewed as a sign that relationships had become qualitatively different.

Siblings varied with respect to how often they interacted with their parents. Contrast the following descriptions provided by two sisters in different families:

> Family holidays and birthdays are held on a rotating basis. Individually, we invite my mother over as we have time, energy, and inclination.

> Once a week for sure, my brother visits on Wednesdays. I'm going tomorrow and taking one of my daughters for overnight. Mom and Dad baby-sit for my sister once a week. So three times a week

they have contact with one of us children, and they come to dinner here every other week. We all go up to Michigan and take cabins in the summer. We've done that for years.

A sister described how she and her two brothers spent time with their father:

My out-of-town brother visits him here. That's all he does. My local brother visits him and takes him to auto races, baseball games, and drives him to see my other brother. I help him with his paperwork for his insurance or any other financial questions he may have. He comes here for dinner occasionally. He has his own routine.

A brother compared his brother's and his own contact with their parents:

On my part, we write to each other every week unless we see them. My parents were down in Kentucky for my daughter's graduation. I call a couple of times a month — two or more phone calls a month. My brother writes less often. I know because he sends the same letter to my parents and me.

The amount of interaction and the degree to which it was planned varied from one family to the next, but most siblings reported that they were in regular contact with their parents.

The occasions that drew family members together varied as well: "I organized the family reunion last year. Before that, family events, weddings would bring us together. One of my brothers is going to organize the reunion this year." Some older families had reached a point where events such as weddings and graduations of grandchildren that previously had brought geographically distant family members together had run their course. More effort was required to insure that family members saw one another. In addition, not being tied to a job meant that most parents could spend relatively long periods of time visiting their nonproximate children:

> My sister calls my mother once a week at least. Mother visits her three-to-four weeks in the winter and one other trip when she stays with her for ten days. She flies Mother to San Francisco to see her great-grand-children.

Telephone and Face-to-Face Interaction

Most siblings, unless they lived with their parents, said that they were in routine telephone contact with them. Those who lived nearby were in frequent contact. Some spoke on the telephone daily:

> My sister talks to her everyday and then I call her on my own. She talks to my other sister and brother quite frequently.

> I call her twice a day, once when I get to work and once when I get home from work. I don't mind catering to my mother. I understand that she's bored and lonely.

> My mother checks in all the time to let me know what she's doing. She'll tell me about what she has done in the course of the day.

> My father does not hesitate to call me and discuss any problems or issues he may have. I call him daily.

Daily calls sometimes were motivated by concern that their parents had survived the night without incident:

> I call them every day. If I didn't get an answer, I'd go over to see if they're alive over there.

> I make sure she's okay. I talk to her on a daily basis, ask her how she's feeling.

> I call her every morning to check on her. I see her every Sunday and some Saturdays

Others talked on the telephone several times a week: "They know I'm here for them. We talk to each other three times a week. I see them every week. There is nothing else to do for them, fortunately."

Nonproximate siblings spoke with their parents less often.[43] Some did not specify a schedule or routine but said that they called their parents regularly:

> We all make an effort to call, I'd say approximately three times a month, and to visit approximately once a year, remembering them, of course, on Mother's Day, Father's Day, their anniversary, birthdays. That's really about it.

> I call at least once a week, sometimes twice.

> My brother does call her a couple of times a month. He talks a long time. He hasn't been up here for five or six years.

Some nonproximate siblings had a specific time to call their parents:

> First Sunday of every month I call, and we talk as long as she wants.

> My brother who lives out of town calls her once a week on Sundays.

> My sister talks to Mother every Sunday, so emotional support is there.

In addition to telephone contact, face-to-face interaction occurred on a regular basis in most of these families. Proximity affected how often it happened. Visiting in parents' homes provided the opportunity for siblings to assist them but was not necessarily the primary reason they were there. Most siblings who lived near their parents visited regularly:

> My sister does go after work, takes a paper over and visits.

> I have Mother over, pick her up to see the kids and have dinner once a week.

> We each have Mother for dinner one night a week. We took her to our place in the country last weekend. In the past years she spent every summer weekend with us.

> I visit a lot. Take him to the cemetery. I clean his refrigerator, do the dishes when I'm there. Mostly he likes me to sit and talk to him. He does get lonesome. One of my sisters writes to him every day.

We try to see that she sees one of us each week.
Weekends she comes to our house or my sister's.
Winter, maybe every two weeks. We take her shopping. We do buy a lot of clothes for her. It's tiresome
for her to try them on. We take her out to lunch or
dinner once a month.

I take her out to dinner once every two weeks. I stop
to see her once a week and call her once a week.

I see my father three times a week. We socialize together once every three weeks.

Siblings who resided with parents or lived very close saw
their parents every day.

On the other hand, those who lived far from their parents
typically saw their parents regularly but not as often:

When I was in Canada, Mother came to live with
me for three months. She didn't like it. My home
now is in Little Rock. I'm here for three weeks just
to visit her.

We were all in Philadelphia in July for my niece's
graduation and Mom went back with my sister to
Georgia to visit. My brother will come in once a week
now to see her. He takes her out to dinner. My other
brother is too far. He did call her a few days ago. He
asked her to come visit him in Japan.

I now visit more often than I used to because of my
father's age. My wife and I visit about twice a year,
and my parents visit us about twice a year.

> My brother who lives in Michigan visits her three-to-four times a year and calls her once every couple of months. They took her on vacation last year, one week.

> I'm always there at Christmas. I'm always there in the summer, a week each time, and I occasionally stop while on business.

> When he comes to Cleveland six times a year, he sees Dad. He calls Dad on the phone every two weeks.

Interaction among members of older families was colored by the parents' advanced age but was not necessarily radically different simply because all had grown older. The exception was when parents required extraordinary care. When parents were capable or "in-between," services were added to and sometimes took the place of more traditional family interaction. Family members did not initiate doing with and for one another when old parents' situations became problematic. Rather, responses to changed circumstances were incorporated into existing patterns of family interaction. Continuous adaptations had been and would continue to be made as family members' circumstances changed through time.

PROVIDING SERVICES

These siblings provided many services to their parents. Siblings who lived near their parents provided more services than those who lived farther away. As was clear in the previous chapter, parents who required round-the-clock, hands-on care received a great deal of assistance from their children, especially if they shared a household. If parents suffered from dementia, moreover, they could offer little in the way of reciprocity except for financial contributions. But what of the self-sufficient and in-between parents?

Rides and Running Errands

How much assistance a proximate sibling provided was a function of whether the parent owned and/or was able to drive an automobile. All but a few of the parents in this study were over the age of 75, many over 80. Some had serious health problems, including problems with their eyes, that made them ineligible or poor drivers. Some were dealing with the aftermath of strokes. Some had cognitive impairments. One clear cohort difference was that some mothers had never learned to drive. Some parents drove but were reported to avoid driving at night or in bad weather. Some siblings stated that they preferred that their parents not drive. A few parents were reported to use public busses or senior citizens vans, and one mother had arranged for a driver.

Parents who did not drive depended, for the most part, on friends and their children to get them to destinations such as the grocery store, medical appointments, shopping, church, recreational activities, and to deliver to them groceries and other items. Siblings often referred to these services as "running errands":

> I take her to the doctor. I take her shopping for the day. Tuesday is shopping day. We take her out to dinner. We realize that she doesn't like to be alone.

I take her grocery shopping, to the doctors, and recreation. Even on weekends, if I'm going with my family, I may drop her off and pick her up later.

My sister and I both do errands. For example, my nephew's birthday is tomorrow, and I bought him a gift for them, and then took Mom to buy birthday cards.

I take her shopping every other Saturday for groceries.

My sister takes her to the doctors most always — and is there a lot — and to dental appointments. I take her shopping every other Saturday for groceries.

Mother doesn't really need that much care. When it comes to shopping, getting glasses, foot doctor, physician, I do that.

Help around the House

Siblings also assisted their parents by doing things for them in their homes. Sisters, but only a few brothers, cooked and cleaned:

When Mom feels good she'll cook and we'll share. A little more lately, I'll make dinner and take something down to her.

I do her cleaning, dusting, vacuuming, and laundry. For Mother's Day my sister had Budget Butler come and help.

I do her sewing, clean up her house, and bring her leftovers.

We both get together and give mother's house a good cleaning about once a month.

My sister is the caregiver. She cleans his house, makes his bed, does his laundry, and makes the majority of his meals.

My sister goes on Monday, strips her bed and remakes it, and takes clothing home to wash. When I go there, I wash there. She always has a lot of wet stuff around because of her problem [incontinence].

Both brothers and sisters said that brothers were more likely to do home repairs and yard work:

When they need help around the house, they call my brother. He's like a landlord.

I work on cars. My mother calls me if someone in the family has a car problem and wants it done right away. My brother takes care of mechanical things and cars. Repairs on house — anyone that's handy.

I visit my father once a week or every two weeks — go shopping, visit, repairs in the house, minor stuff.

If she wants something moved in the house, she'll call one of us. If she wants flowers planted, she'll call me. I'm the gardener in the family.

> My sister's the one who says I'll be over with the kids to cut the grass.

> When we visit we do little things around the house and farm, like chop wood, fence fixing. Nothing else.

Some siblings provided assistance to parents who were snowbirds or went on long vacations:

> My father owns a farm, which has been in his family for 100 years. During the winter my brother does whatever has to be done to keep the farm in shape by contacting the people who have leased it. Also the biggest thing he has done is visit and keep in contact with my father's sister, who is ill. That relieves my father of much pressure. He packs and unpacks the car when they go and come from Florida. He takes care of mail, looks after their house when they are in Florida. When they are in Indianapolis, he visits them once a week at least. He doesn't do anything for them when they are in Indianapolis.

Of course, siblings who lived with their parents performed a variety of services; however, unless the parent was very dependent, these adult children also received benefits that came with sharing household responsibilities.

Finally, there were also parents who lived in apartments, condominiums, or retirement communities, who did not require many of these services.

Care in Time of Illness

Siblings reported providing care when parents were recovering from operations or were ill:

> During my father's last illness, I picked up my mother every morning to take her to the hospital. Then we ate lunch and went shopping.

> He had what they thought was a heart attack three years ago. I had to go out there every day to make sure he wouldn't leave the hospital.

> Last year when my father was ill, I spent maybe a total of five months [with my parents] in Florida.

> After the automobile accident, my folks went to my sister's place to recover.

> When my mother was in the hospital, I would go every day and rinse out her nightgown, went to her apartment to take care of her plants, and kept her money.

> I came when Dad was in the hospital to stay with mother so that she had medication.

> She had a test two weeks ago and needed liquids. I stayed over night, and another time I stayed four nights.

> When mother was hospitalized, my brother and his wife took care of the hospital. I went in when she came home and stayed with her until I thought she could stay alone.

When Dad had a hip replacement seven or eight years ago, he had it in Cleveland, and he stayed with us afterwards. It gave him time to recuperate and took the burden off Mom.

I arranged for her to have a lens implant about six months ago. She stayed here for about 9 weeks after that.

Sisters were more likely than brothers to report providing this type of care.

Money Management

Incomes of old parents can be quite complex if they come from various sources. Many siblings indicated that one member of the sibling group was the "executor" for the family, having become one either when a parent died or before the fact in anticipation of a parent's death. In addition, puzzling through medical bills and health insurance forms was challenging. Some siblings indicated that they had assumed these tasks for their parents:

My sister handles financial things. She looks after bills.

I've taken over her financial affairs. I have power of attorney. I pay her bills.

Usually one of us stops there once a day. Maybe my brother goes more because he handles bills. Mom needs a lot of help with money.

I just helped him with his taxes.

Lately I've been helping her with her checkbook. She's getting forgetful.

Complicated bills I help her with — Medicare, complicated phone bills.

Managing money was not as clearly related to gender, although when brothers and husbands were available, they often assumed this task.

Financial Assistance

Very few of the informants indicated that they were giving money to their parents. In the United States legislation passed in the 1970s effectively instituted a guaranteed minimum income for all older Americans. Those who receive very low or no Social Security benefits are eligible for Supplemental Security Income. Those not eligible for Medicare receive Medicaid if their incomes are low. In addition, other pension plans have come to fruition. As a result, the percentage of the old who are poor has declined significantly.[44] In fact, for the old whose families are very poor, their guaranteed income may provide the primary element of security to younger relatives if they are also poor.

An exception to this rosy picture was a very old woman who had taken up residence in her early 70s in an apartment hotel that had gentrified in the ensuing years. A sister made sure that her mother's rent was paid, regardless of whether her three siblings contributed. A brother in another family gave his very old mother money every month to help her cover expenses: "My brother sends my mother $150 a month of his own money." A brother whose parents had been divorced when he was in high school claimed to support his 80-year-old mother. One brother who, with another brother, operated a business that their father had founded, was credited by a third brother with helping "my father substantially. He gives Father a salary and makes him feel part of the business." Brothers were more likely than sisters to provide direct financial assistance to their parents.

Other siblings indicated that they enhanced the quality of their parents' lives by paying for specific things:

> Financially, my sister and I do everything 50/50; for example, a hearing aid that wasn't covered by Medicare. We do extras, take her to dinner.

> I'm her financial advisor and lawyer, get all her tax information together; but an accountant does the tax return and I pay for it.

On the whole, money was not something that the siblings mentioned often or directly. There were oblique references, however, to financial arrangements; for example, parents' houses that were now in siblings' names and parents renting condominiums from siblings. As noted above, moreover, many of the families included "executors."

Services Tailored to Parents

Siblings were in a position to act in ways that they knew their parents would appreciate. Often they did things that formal service providers would not be able to provide.[45] Siblings treated their parents as unique individuals:

I see that priests get to her and communion is brought.

I went with her to visit some relatives in Phoenix and LA. We had a marvelous time, and it was the first time she smiled since my father died.

Every Saturday when my mother is in town, it's a pattern we've fallen into. I take her to visit her 101-years-old sister in a nursing home.

My sister took Mother to Bermuda after she recuperated from the fall that resulted in a hip fracture.

I got a court injunction against a would-be suitor.

I plan to take him to the homecoming football game at Ohio State.

One of my brothers used to stop and visit my father a lot after Mother died. He and Dad used to drink together.

I take Mother shopping because it's our time together. There's a reason why I take her. She and Dad fight and she likes to window shop and he won't let her. So she rarely goes shopping with Dad.

I get them The Plain Dealer and have it delivered to their house in Florida. I call them every week. I want to make sure they know we're here and whatever we can do for them we will.

I bring my father fifteen cans of beer and two fifths of vodka every week.

He takes her to his summer home in Canada one or two weeks a year. It's been difficult for him, but he has done it. Mom decides when she wants to go, usually sometime in July. So far he has managed.

My out-of-town brother calls her every Sunday morning and provides her with symphony tickets.

We're having a party for Mother's 80th birthday.

John has on occasion made special trips to Cleveland. My father was honored at the Business School, and my brother made a special trip to attend the banquet.

Unlike those who offer formal services to elderly clients, siblings knew what special services their parents were likely to appreciate, as well as what assistance they found intrusive. Armed with this knowledge, they contributed to their parents' well-being in seemingly minor but, in fact, important ways that formal service providers could not. Furthermore, to place these contributions under the rubric of "parent care" would be wrong. Instead, they are the kinds of things that family members do to confirm that they know well and care about one another.

Siblings, then, performed a variety of services for their parents. Which ones depended on their geographic proximity to their parents, their parents' circumstances, and their gender. Parent's health status was an important factor, especially for those who required extraordinary care, but the most important factor for "in-between" and capable parents was whether they drove an automobile. Proximate siblings incorporated into their schedules transporting parents to church or medical appointments or ran errands for them, such as grocery and clothes shopping. Distant siblings were at a disadvantage in that they were unable to accommodate the needs of parents who required transportation or someone at hand for other services. They did, however, provide services that were less routine or that arose as emergencies.

ADDING IN-LAWS

The focus on relationships among family members meant that siblings were thought of as tied not only to their parents and one another but also to their own spouses and their siblings' spouses. Predictably, siblings reported that the expectations of their partners sometimes conflicted with their own and those of their parents, sisters, and brothers. Given the impact that a husband or wife has on a sibling's involvement with her or his parents, ties between in-laws have received very little attention in the research literature on older families.[46] The exception is wives of men who have no sisters. In the literature on primary caregivers, they are depicted as filling in for their nonexistent sisters-in-law by performing the filial duties that fall to their husbands.[47] Focusing on family relationships rather than caregivers leads to a somewhat different conclusion

Even though many of the siblings' husbands and wives had known their parents- and siblings-in-laws for extended periods of time, their ties remained mediated. That is, the very existence of their relationships depended on the sibling to whom they were married. This was most evident in the typical response to the question that asked respondents to tell what their spouses and each of their siblings' spouses did with and for parents. When a sibling was divorced, respondents dismissed the question as inappropriate by saying, for example, "and my sister is divorced" or "my ex-wife is out of town." Former in-laws had no obligation to one another:

My sister's first husband was very close to Father. After the divorce, Father missed him.

My husband has done nothing in the last year since we are in the process of getting a divorce.

In some cases parents made the decision to end the relationship. A divorced brother who had no children said, "I think my ex-wife would like to have stayed in contact, but my parents discouraged it." Even when cordial relationships were maintained, in most cases former children-in-law were expected to do no more than visit their former parents-in-law or, if they had special skills, to respond when asked.[48]

Like the siblings themselves, the contributions of spouses were "gender appropriate."[49] Husbands were reported to perform typically masculine tasks for their parents-in-law:

My brother-in-law handles finances. He does it all: pays the bills, insurance, medical. He helps with Medicare and Blue Cross.

Janet's husband painted their kitchen, mows the lawn. Jane's husband does minor house repairs, will plant flowers. He gives my father a lot of moral support and financial advice. Alice's husband repairs Father's car. Susan's husband runs errands for Father.

My husband helps with stocks and financial matters, and maybe if the mower got stuck he'll help her.

My brother-in-law is very helpful, supportive, kind. He'll do whatever he can for her, whatever is needed. He took over stock management, helped her with income tax, does repairs at her place if needed.

My brother-in-law does minor, household repairs that she can't do. He shovels snow, plows the driveway.

My husband takes care of some of her money and advises us. His biggest service is providing a home and being even-tempered about it. He's a walking saint.

Husbands were likely to have different skills from their wives (but not from brothers-in-law) and to be more capable than an elderly father in performing traditionally male tasks.

Daughters-in-law apparently were expected to perform tasks that are associated with the female-gender role:

My wife has provided sympathy and emotional support. She talks to my father on the phone and writes letters.

I guess it would be easier for me [if I had a sister]. If she were around here, she could do the shopping, etc. The way it works out, my wife does all these things for her.

My brothers' wives take her shopping, which is important to her. John's wife goes to lunch with her.

As a matter of fact, I think my wife has taken the role of a sister in terms of letter writing and keeping me and my brothers informed of events and that.

> This is my second wife. We've been married six years.
> My brother's wife knows him better. She helped him
> sort out my mother's clothes. She's acted more as an
> advisor from a woman's point of view.

> My wife has the same contact that I have. We do a
> lot of things together. We go together. She cooks for
> her often, takes her food. What I've done, she's done
> equally. As far as my sister-in-law, geography prevents
> that. She writes. She's the communicator. She'll call
> up or she'll write.

Wives, then, participated in stereotypically female ways
just as husbands participated in stereotypically male ways.
Geographic proximity also played a part in how often in-
laws interacted and in how much assistance an in-law child
could provide to a parent-in-law.

Not all wives and husbands, however, participated in
visiting or providing services. There was a great deal of
variation with respect to the way spouses participated in
their in-law families. Many of the in-law relationships had
existed for twenty years or more. How children-in-law participated in the family had been well established before their
parents-in-law became elderly.

In some cases marriages had signaled a sibling's with-
drawal from the family of origin:

> When she got married she embraced her husband and
> her children and became more distant.

> His wife is nuts and refused to let him have any con-
> tact with the family.

A widowed sister explained why her brother "can't do anything" for their mother:

> His wife makes decisions that he has to abide by. It has come to me to do most of everything for my mother. It just worked out this way because of my brother's wife.

In other cases ties between a sibling and a sibling-in-law were less than cordial:[50]

> We spend more time with my wife's family than mine. My sister is jealous, and one night it erupted, and she doesn't speak to my wife anymore.

> We don't socialize. Her husband is a little difficult.

> When my father was terminally ill, my wife had free time, is a very compassionate person, and sat with him often. I think my sister was jealous of this in a way, because she was employed and couldn't be there as much.

In still other cases, the parent and in-law-child were described as not being fond of one another:

> My wife and my parents never got along well.

> If temporary, she'd come stay with me. She wouldn't relish living in my house. My husband's temper tantrums upset her.

> Mother never had any relationship with her sons-in-law.

As far as my brother's wife, there's not closeness at all with her. Mother never really feels welcome there.

My sister's husband is a constant thorn in my mother's side. He constantly puts her down. He's tactless and says what he thinks, usually at the wrong time.

At the other extreme were in-law children who became active members of their in-law families:

All three of the sisters-in-law, all three of them, have been close to Mother. My wife will go to Cleveland, perhaps spend three or four days with Mother twice a year, in addition to what we do as a couple.

My mother and my wife are very good friends. They talk in addition to what I do, at least once a week, sometimes two or three times a week.

My husband takes on my mother as if she were his own; he's very thoughtful of her.

My husband does little and big repairs and car repairs. They're close like a father and son.

My husband is like another son. He never argues. He listens. She loves him very much. My brother's wife is wonderful, like another daughter. She thinks of her almost as much as her own mother, who is still alive.

My wife calls my mother often. She gets along well with her.

Relationships among in-law children are also a consideration: "After I was married our husbands really liked each other and all four of us became very close." When meeting parents' needs became an issue, spouses who had warm relationships with their parents- and siblings-in-law were more likely to be involved and supportive because they were integral parts of the family into which they had married.

In between these two extremes were in-laws who ranged from tolerating to liking and respecting one another. These ties were described more succinctly and as if there was recognition that there could be more problems than there were:

> My parents are not as close to my brother's wife as they are to my wife, but she likes them and helps them when necessary.

> My wife is very supportive of my mother. We have her for holidays and birthday parties.

> My husband is very encouraging about having my parents come to visit.

> My brother's wife writes letters to Mother; nothing else.

> My sister's husband would help her up steps. He is a helpful, supportive person.

> Both sons-in-law are kind and supportive people. They don't do concrete services but do suggest that we have Mother over and occasionally suggest a small gift.

These in-law children helped when called upon but were less likely to initiate activities or to become actively involved because of their moderate attachment to their parents-in-law.

Spouses, much like siblings, were similarly affected by gender and geographic proximity. Their attachment to the members of the families into which they had married was an additional ingredient. Not being privy to the earlier negotiation of in-law relationships, it is impossible to know who was responsible for the place they now occupied on the continuum. Only the consequences are evident.

This chapter identified what siblings did with and for their old parents. Siblings were in contact with parents and provided a variety of services. Geographic proximity of the sibling to her or his parent affected the amount of interaction and the circumstances under which it occurred. Some services tended to be more the province of one gender than the other, so that sisters or brothers were more likely to perform them. This was also the case for siblings' spouses, but how involved spouses were also was a function of their relationships with their parents- and siblings-in-law.

Most of this chapter focused on individual siblings, belying the earlier promise to focus on relationships rather than on roles. Bringing spouses into the frame, however, points to the fact that decisions about how to interact with members of the original family were not simply a sibling's alone. Rather, married siblings linked their spouses to members of their original family. Relationships among in-laws depended a great deal on how they felt about one another. Spouses influenced siblings' interactions with their parents and their siblings. In the next chapter the value of thinking of families as a set of relationships becomes more apparent.

Chapter Four

Dividing Family Labor
in Sibling Groups

DURING THE INTERVIEWS respondents not only recounted what they and their siblings did with and for their parents but also why a brother or sister did more or less than another and why each of them did specific things. These reasons often but not always were presented without rancor — as simply how things had fallen into place. Siblings took into account eight attributes or circumstances to explain their own participation and that of their sisters and brothers.[51] In most research these would be variables that described adult children — for example, geographical distance from parents.[52] Because this project focused on groups of siblings, such attributes also describe relations among family members. The siblings used not only absolute standing (e.g., how many miles each sibling lived from the parents) but relative standing (e.g., which of them lived closer or closest) to explain each sibling's participation in family labor. That is, how two unrelated adult children who both live fifty miles from their respective parents are involved in the family labor of meeting parents' needs is a function not only of that absolute distance but also of where their respective siblings live. One may live closest, the other farthest from their respective parents and, as a result, participate differently. Relative distances, rather than actual distances, from parents become the focus when family relationships rather than roles are considered.

The order in which the eight attributes are discussed below is somewhat arbitrary. First addressed are gender and relative geographic proximity to parents because of their powerful effect on the types of interaction and services rendered. As noted in the previous chapter, some tasks are more likely to be performed by sisters or brothers and some types of family labor cannot be accomplished from a distance.[53] Next are mutable attributes. Those, like employment status, which can be changed, are discussed first, followed by attributes that cannot be changed as easily, if at all — for example, marital status and birth order.

Each attribute is discussed separately; however, siblings considered combinations of the attributes on which they differed — for example, gender differences *and* geographic distance of each sibling from the parents *and* age of each sibling's children. Furthermore, differences among siblings are emphasized in this chapter, but it is important to keep in mind that in some families there were no differences on at least some of these attributes. The data included in this chapter, then, are primarily from siblings who differed on the attribute being discussed.

In this chapter the significance of size and gender composition of sibling networks becomes evident. Discussion of relative attributes requires knowing "relative to whom." For each data excerpt the respondent's gender, as well as the gender and number of his or her siblings, is noted, a practice that continues for the remainder of the book.

GENDER AS A RELATIVE ATTRIBUTE

Gender can be used as a relative attribute only in mixed-gender sibling groups. Sixty-six sibling groups were mixed gender: fifty lone-sister and sixteen pairs of sisters who had at least one brother. It is apparent in data cited in this and previous chapters that, when it was an option, gender was used to explain and justify differences in participation.

Some sisters indicated that their brothers always had been given preferential treatment:

> I was very angry about my mother giving him money, but she always showed partiality towards her sons. I was just a girl. They had all of the brains. She had really no respect for me since she felt girls weren't equal to boys. (*Sister with two brothers*)

Sisters, but not brothers, sometimes indicated that they were not necessarily pleased that duties were assigned on the basis of gender:

> Because I'm the girl. They think it's the girl's responsibility. That bothers me, but I do it because they need me; and if the tables were turned, I would want someone to do it for me, and that's just the way it is. (*Sister with four brothers*)

Another sister was more resistive but, nevertheless, accepted that it was her role:

> One thing changed is that being the only girl I got dumped all the housework. Now that I'm an adult and if I fall back on the household duties, they will pick up and help with the slack. (*Sister with five brothers*)

She now expected her brothers "to help her" with housework but not to take responsibility. Differences in the way brothers and sisters participated, then, were rooted in family histories that emphasized gender differences.

Both brothers and sisters in some mixed-gender sibling groups said that the mother-daughter dyad was important in their family:

> And being an only daughter, I am very close to my mom. It just fell into place. (*Sister with two brothers*)

> My sister, the only daughter, is a confidante to Mother. (*Brother with one sister and two brothers*)

> It has to do with gender. Mom feels more comfortable if I take her to the doctor. She discusses feelings with me. Ours is a more personal relationship. (*Sister with two brothers*)

> The relationship with a daughter is closer. Daughters are more patient. Therefore, another sister might provide more patience for Mother. (*Brother with a sister and a brother*)

> My sister is close emotionally to Mom because they share housekeeping interests. (*Brother with one sister and three brothers*)

On the other hand, some siblings in mixed-gender sibling groups pointed to the father-son dyad in the family as important:

> My dad and my brother were always very close. For example, when my sister or I were late getting in, my father didn't care; but when my brother was even one minute late, my father was pacing the floor. (*Sister with one sister and one brother*)

> My brother has been very close to my father. Closer than I am. They've always worked together in repair and odd jobs around the house. (*Sister with one brother*)

Same-gender intergenerational dyads, then, were imbued with meaning in some mixed-gender sibling groups and became important with respect to who did what with and for old parents.

Differences in gender roles also were cited as important. A gender role is "a set of expectations about what behaviors are appropriate for people of one gender."[54] A sister indicated that there was "appropriate" differentiation on the basis of gender in her family:

> My brother and my husband share repairs. They both put in the garage door opener. My husband may paint and wallpaper. My brother put in a faucet. On decorating, my mom usually turns to me. I guess I am the daughter. I put in more time, conversation, and personal care. It's just the gender thing. I don't know about cars. My brother doesn't know about decorating. I can't do repairs, but my husband and brother can. My brother is willing, but more of the personal just falls on me. There's a whole lot of work in personal care, you know: cleaning, sitting, and listening. My brother has more influence with Dad, like getting him to sign papers, because Dad doesn't think women are capable. (*Sister with one brother*)

Her brother agreed:

> I can't think of any reason other than it's my mother's wishes. If there's plumbing to be done, she would call me, not my sister. She would relegate tasks as to what's to be performed. (*Brother with one sister*)

Relegating was based on what the mother considered "gender appropriate." A sister with three brothers considered herself better qualified than her brothers to clean and to listen to their father:

> I clean my father's apartment. He visits me every other Sunday. I listen to him. I'm the only one I think that he is able to share things with. (*Sister with three brothers*)

A brother explained that he and his sister did different things for their recently widowed father:

> My sister has come in for intervals of several weeks at a time. She has trained my father to care for the house. I've tried to include him in our family activities. (*Brother with one sister*)

Sisters and brothers in mixed-gender sibling groups performed tasks for their parents that were "gender appropriate," commensurate with gender roles.

Personal care for infirm parents also broke down along gender lines. One sister explained that only a woman would be appropriate to provide personal care for her mother and that she, as the only daughter, was carrying a heavy load:

> I am over three or four times a day. But I just don't trust anyone but family, and it should be a woman for privacy. (*Sister with one brother*)

Her brother agreed that it was unfair, but as a man he saw little that he could do:

> That's the unfair part of it. Right now we don't divide it equally. She lives there, next door, and she's retired; so there is proximity and time. There's little a son can do for an invalid mother. I really am restricted in what I can do. (*Brother with one sister*)

Other siblings also indicated that, when it came to personal care, sisters and brothers were not interchangeable:

> Right now I'm freer to do it than my sister, but my mother wouldn't feel so comfortable with me bathing her. (*Brother with one sister and one brother*)

> My dad would take care of her or, if I would be home, I would. She wouldn't allow my brothers to bathe her or anything like that. (*Sister with two brothers*)

Although the effects of gender roles were not limited to mixed-gender sibling groups, only in these groups was it possible to use gender differences as an explanation for why one sibling rather than another performed specific tasks.

RELATIVE PROXIMITY TO PARENTS

As noted in the previous chapter, distance between siblings and parents was a very important consideration in what siblings did with and for their parents. The farther from a parent a sibling lived, the more difficult it was to visit regularly, to have firsthand knowledge of a parent's situation, and to provide services such as transportation and grocery shopping.[55] Siblings rarely lived the same distance from their parents. One almost always lived closer. Distance from parents was invoked whether it was minimal or great.

The effect of distance was obvious when one or more siblings were in close proximity to parents while others lived far away. If parents required daily or weekly services, the closer sibling provided them:

My mother always calls me first. Everyone else is out of town. She isn't going to call them out of town. I'm the only one available for any kind of emergencies or visits and everything else. (*Sister with two sisters and one brother*)

In terms of division, my brother does most of it because he's there. I stay in touch by phone. (*Brother with one brother*)

My brother [who left town after high school] has never been a help. Both my husband and I stayed in the city with our own parents. Both our mothers died young, so we're the caretakers. My husband's sisters moved away with their husbands, so for forty years we've been doing it. (*Sister with one brother*)

My other brother is limited in helping her because he doesn't live here. When he lived here, he was the best of the bunch. (*Brother with two brothers*)

Even when two or more siblings lived nearby, a difference of a few minutes or miles was often given as an explanation for why one sibling visited more often or was more likely to be called by parents in an emergency:

I probably do more because I'm closer. There's no reason for my sister to come across town when I am over here closer to my mother. (*Brother with one sister*)

My mother would call my brother first because he is closer. When my dad had a stroke, she called him first. For emergencies it would be my brother as well if a problem occurred. He's closer. I'm an hour away. (*Sister with one brother*)

My brother, I would say, spends more time with my mother than I do. It's advantageous for him to do so. He lives a little closer. (*Brother with one brother*)

I'm the one who does the handiwork, but it's not too much since I'm the closer one. I wouldn't expect my brother to come twenty miles to fix a light switch. (*Brother with one brother*)

Geographically she would call me if she had an emergency. When she fell and went into the hospital she called me. My sister is thirty miles away. (*Sister with one sister and one brother*)

Coresidence with parents was the most extreme case of being the closer or closest sibling.[56] Regardless of whether others lived nearby or far away, a sibling who lived with parent(s) was described as doing more:

There is no organization of contributions. It falls into place because my brother lives there. (*Sister with one brother*)

I somehow feel if they didn't live together we'd find some way to divide the work more evenly. (*Sister with one sister*)

In some families siblings lived equidistant from their parents. There was a variety of ways in which this occurred. In some families everyone lived close to one another. In one family, described in a previous chapter, the mother and brother recently had moved into the sister's home:

> When my mother and brother lived in their other home,
> I had to go over there almost every day because my
> brother works. Once they moved here, three months
> ago, things are great. (*Sister with one brother*)

Combining households eliminated the difference in proximity to the mother for this sister-brother pair. In another
family the brother and sister lived close to one another in
Cleveland but several hours from their parents who lived
in a small town in Pennsylvania. When their father called
to tell them that he had been involved in an automobile accident but was "home and all right,"

> my brother went the next day because of our concern
> and also because, being an attorney, he wanted to make
> sure Dad's license wouldn't be taken away. I went to
> see them that weekend. We thought if we went together
> right after the accident, they'd be alarmed. (*Sister with
> one brother*)

This brother and sister, because they lived the same distance
from their parents, could not use geographic proximity to
determine who would go first.

In another family two sisters resided, respectively, 110
miles and 1200 miles from their parents. Even though one
sister lived considerably closer than the other, they agreed
that neither of them lived close enough to visit often and
that it was appropriate to rely on someone near their parents
to keep them informed:

> We have a close friend who goes in once a month and
> straightens out their checkbook. He goes to the same
> church. He said it wasn't too bad yet, and he said to
> hold tight. He's a good friend. (*Sister with one sister*)

Difference in proximity, then, is not always objective but a matter of definition. When their parents were in a serious automobile accident, however, the reason given for their recuperating at the home of one sister rather than the other was that she lived closer.

Relative Employment Status

and Job Characteristics

Women's increased participation in the labor force alarms those who fear that daughters' jobs compete with their assisting old parents.[57] In fact, this study initially was designed to address this issue by focusing on the effects of employment for pairs of sisters whose employment status differed.[58] Fewer studies have explored how jobs affect men's interaction with old parents[59] — in large part because, for them, employment is assumed to be mandatory while, for women, it is viewed as voluntary (however inaccurate this assumption may be). In addition, men are not expected to assist old parents because family care is presumed to be "women's work."[60] Still fewer studies have explored how relative employment status in sibling groups affects involvement with old parents. These data can illuminate all three of these issues.

In the United States, as in most Western countries, there is a dual labor market. Specific jobs are occupied almost exclusively either by men or women, so that the job itself is gendered: there are "men's jobs" and there are "women's jobs." In the wake of civil rights legislation that prohibited job discrimination on the basis of gender, there have been some changes, but there continues to be a strong association between gender and job title. A very small number of job titles continues to describe employed women, while men are distributed among a huge number. In addition, men's jobs tend to be more lucrative than women's and are more likely to have career ladders that include an expectation that their occupants will move where the next step on the ladder dictates. As a result employees are likely to relinquish both wages and a position on a ladder when they leave such a job. Women's jobs pay less and have short ladders, characteristics that make comparable jobs easier to find. Men's jobs, moreover, are more likely to include longer hours and travel.

Most men expect to join the labor force upon completion of their education and to remain employed until they retire. More women expect to move in and out of the labor force as family and personal proclivities dictate. Although currently more women are on career paths, as a group they continue to be much more flexible than men with respect to labor-force participation. Women, not men, take parental and family leave. Men who work part-time and in contingency jobs are likely to do so at the conclusion of their work life, women throughout their lives.[61]

For all of these reasons, it is a mistake to assume that the only difference between employed sisters and brothers is their gender. Whether the dual labor market is fair is an important topic that is beyond the scope of this book. Instead, discussion is confined to its consequences for how family labor is divided.

Siblings differed with respect to whether they worked, when they worked, and how many hours they worked. Relative employment status was used as a rationale for what members of sibling groups did for their parents; but just as significant were features of jobs, including degree of job flexibility, knowledge and skills required to perform them, and access to networks through jobs.

Employed vs. Nonemployed

The nonemployed siblings in a group were likely to do the things that needed to be done during their siblings' work hours: "I am more available during the day because my sister works at a day-care center. I'm retired" (*Brother with one sister*). A brother described how his nonemployed sister participated differently from her two brothers:

> My brother is away most of the time and is available only on weekends. My sister is home and can do things and make calls. I work and am free evenings and weekends. (*Brother with one sister and one brother*)

A brother pointed out that he and his sister did more than his employed siblings:

> Well, of course, my sister and I feel that the youngest siblings should do more than they are now, but they're restricted by distance and by job limitations. We're retired. We can do more. My brother, who's the businessman in Painesville, can't be shooting over here to Cleveland once a week. (*Brother with one sister and two brothers*)

One sister said that now that she was retired, there had been a shift in how she and her employed sister divided responsibilities:

> My sister lives a little closer, so it used to be that she saw Mother more often, but since I'm retired it's about the same. (*Sister with one sister and one brother*)

Employment brings financial remuneration, and nonemployed siblings pointed to the wages earned by their employed siblings:

> My sister has more money financially. I have more time.
> I would spend money on them if I had a job and extra
> money, but I know I would have less time to spend with
> them. This way I have more time and less money. That's
> all. Because she works, she has more money to spend
> on the nice things in life for them — for example, a
> picture for their wall. (*Sister with one sister*)

A member of a group of four siblings whose mother received
financial assistance from them distinguished between those
who were employed and those who were not:

> My younger brother and I, the working members,
> would pick it up as we have been doing. We all defray
> costs, but he and I have been doing most of it. (*Sister
> with one sister and two brothers*)

Employed siblings said that, during their work hours, they
depended on their nonemployed siblings to do things with
and for the parents. Both employed and nonemployed siblings said that their siblings' jobs affected the kinds of things
they did for their parents. If old parents required financial
assistance, employed siblings were more likely than their
nonemployed siblings to provide it.

Job Flexibility

Being employed, however, did not necessarily preclude
siblings assisting parents during their hours on the job.
The fact that the parents in this study were almost all over
the age of 75 meant that, for the most part, brothers and
some sisters had been in the labor force for a considerable
length of time and had benefits associated with seniority. One brother stated that he and his three brothers had

"reached an age and position so that we can get away as needed. None of us has to punch a time clock." A sister explained,

> I'm at the point in terms of what I'm doing that I'm not carrying life and death situations. If the need was there, family responsibilities come first. I've been real careful about professional commitments, so I could be flexible and come if I needed to. My other sister just started working. She doesn't have the flexibility I have. (*Sister with two sisters and one brother*)

Some siblings reported having no problem taking time away from their jobs. One brother, who had recently lost his job as a repairman, said:

> When I had the job, then I could do anything for them — I had a lot of slack time and could run errands for them. When I was out on a job and it was close, I stopped in to do things for them. I was taking Dad for walks during my lunch hour when I worked. (*Brother with two brothers*)

Another respondent reported: "I am flexible to some extent. I am in supervision, so I just delegate my job. My brother, too — he's a salesman and part-owner of his company — has flexibility." Asked how often he had actually taken time off, he replied:

> It may be probably six times a year. My parents know what hours we normally work, and if they need assistance, they try to schedule it as late as possible in the day. (*Brother with two brothers*)

One brother claimed: "I do what has to be done. I can arrange things at work or do it on Saturday or after work, or I take the time off" (*Brother with one brother*).

Others said that self-employment provided flexibility (although one brother cited self-employment itself as a drawback). A self-employed respondent said, "I'm more available [than my brother] since I work for myself" (*Brother with one brother*). As a previously self-employed respondent explained,

> I could leave here if I had to. It's not as flexible as when we had our own business. Now we have other bosses. It used to be a lot more flexible. She had a little more difficult time when my father was alive. He was in bad shape his last five years. She'd need help with him if he fell or he needed to be lifted. She couldn't do it alone. At the time the three of us brothers were in the same office and we'd just say, "Which one's going?" (*Brother with two brothers*)

One of his brothers said about him, "His schedule is more flexible than mine, and he is more accessible than I am, and so he will take her to the doctor." Another brother reported that his job was "pretty demanding" in terms of hours but that his time was also "quite flexible," so that he was able to take his parents for medical appointments during the day (*Brother with one brother*).

Some siblings were teachers, a profession that ostensibly includes summers off. One brother who, along with his wife, cared for his frail mother in their home, said: "If I had a fifty-week-a-year job, the whole situation would be pretty sticky. I'm off summers. We have flexibility" (*Brother with two brothers*). A different brother, comparing himself to his only brother, said, "He's in a very regimented corporate work setting. Me, I have a very flexible academic setting." Another brother explained:

Well, the fact that I'm working obviously puts time limits on what I can do, not necessarily too narrow or too strict. I just say, "I'm gonna be gone three weeks. I hope you don't mind." (*Brother with two brothers*)

Jobs also made siblings easy to get hold of if their parents had a problem: "They could reach him easier during the day because he is in an office and I'm out in the field all day" (*Brother with one brother*). Another explained that his brother would probably be called in an emergency "since he's in the office all day" (*Brother with one brother*). Holding a job, then, did not necessarily preclude assisting a parent during traditional work hours. There was more flexibility than is apparent when only employment status is considered. Degree of job flexibility was a relative attribute when more than one sibling was employed.[62]

Knowledge and Networks

In addition to the money they generated, some siblings reported that their jobs provided knowledge and access to other people, both of which they were able to use to their parents' advantage.[63] One brother, for example, said that his brother "understands legal problems if they need help" (*Brother with three brothers*). Another said that his mother would call him for help with investments because that was his field (*Brother with one brother*). Jobs provided a variety of skills that were described as useful:

My brother, the priest, part of his line of work is dealing with sick people and old people. Then again, my mother's not sick, but he understands the type of problems an older person has. (*Brother with three brothers*)

> He's a salesman. If something has to be resolved over the phone, he'll take care of it. As a matter of fact, this last incident with the doctor, he handled that. He's good with people. I kind of shy away from that. (*Brother of two brothers*)

Jobs also tied siblings to others who provided advice and assistance:

> He's a physician. I've involved him in seeking out medical and paramedical help, counseling; and in times of financial, business things with my mother, he can call on his friends. (*Brother with one brother*)

> My sister tries to help them in this way because she works at a hospital and has access to many different kinds of doctors. My sister seeks out specialists or new doctors for them. (*Brother with one sister and one brother*)

> I think probably in each case that having access to resources through our work is an advantage. I know lots of doctors and can help my parents make sure they get care. (*Brother with three brothers*)

Siblings saw relative advantages in terms of skills and contacts acquired through their jobs that were or might prove useful to their parents. Unless siblings held the same jobs, they were likely to have different knowledge and access to different networks.

Within a sibling group, then, it was not simply a matter of who was employed and who was not. Whose job was more flexible, whether the knowledge associated with an occupation was useful for an issue at hand, and the utility of a network associated with a specific position were also important considerations.

Relative Marital Status

and In-law Ties

Differences in marital status between or among siblings had many ramifications for the way family labor was divided. First, within a group of siblings, the unmarried, if any, were more likely to live with their parents. Some had always lived with them:

> I've lived here. I have no family of my own. This is my family. If I were married and had a wife and four kids, there's no way I could do what I'm doing now for my parents. (*Brother with a sister and a brother*)

> She's there on the spot and she's single. (*Sister with one sister*)

> It's his choice to live there for free. He has a built-in wife with my mother. She does his meals and laundry. He's very dependent on my parents and they are on him, too. (*Sister with two brothers*)

Some had chosen to live with their parents more recently due to their parent's health status or their own economic circumstances or a combination of the two. A divorced sister had moved in with her mother in a small town in Pennsylvania six months earlier after her father died. Her married brother lived nearby:

> My mother is very concerned about my ruining my
> life. If I were to have stayed in Cleveland, I wouldn't
> have been happy worrying about her. My house was a
> heavy drain on me because I hadn't been working for
> a year; so it worked out well financially for me to sell
> my house and move in here. (*Sister with one brother*)

Even when unmarried siblings did not co-reside with
parents, they and their married siblings cited absence of a
spouse as the reason for their doing more:

> Basically, it's more on my [divorced] sister because
> she's single, lives in Chicago, and can be more flexible.
> (*Brother with one sister*)

> My [divorced] brother goes more often because he
> doesn't have much social life and has more time. He
> feels more responsible for them. (*Brother with one
> brother*)

> She has, for the past couple of years, been having the
> family over for holidays — Easter, Christmas. She en-
> joys it. She's been divorced for three years, and maybe
> this fills the gap a little. (*Sister with one sister*)

A recent widow told why she visited her mother more often
than her married siblings did:

> Everyone tells me not to go so much. I feel that I'm
> alone so much. Maybe I understand it more than the
> others. It is something that weighs on me. I go to visit
> her on my way to or from something. It is very depress-
> ing to go there and listen to the complaints. (*Sister with
> one sister and two brothers*)

Siblings in groups that included both the married and the
single, then, cited this difference as a reason why unmar-

ried siblings interacted with parents more often than the married.

When more than one sibling were married, relative support of spouses was an issue. In the research literature daughters-in-law, especially those married to men who have no sisters, are described as substituting for "missing" daughters.[64] As noted earlier, in the families included in this study, it was clear that not all in-laws were supportive and that the degree of support varied within families. Again, not absolute but relative support was the issue addressed by the siblings.

When asked to describe the contributions of those who had married into the family, siblings often contrasted their participation:

> My parents are not as close to my brother's wife as they are to my wife, but she likes them and helps them when necessary. (*Brother with one brother*)

> My brother's wife — forget it. My other brother's wife — a step above forget it. (*Sister with two brothers*)

> My wife has provided sympathy and emotional support. She talks to my father on the phone and writes letters. My brother's wife does less than my wife, but she is warm and kind, and I'm sure her contacts with them are positive. (*Brother with one brother*)

Relative marital status, then, went beyond whether some siblings were married, others not. Those who were married tied an additional person to the family to help, at least potentially, with family labor. Spouses, however, did not participate uniformly. They ranged in their support from very helpful to obstructive. Within a family, support from in-laws for their old parents-in-laws was often described in relative terms.

RELATIVE RESPONSIBILITY

FOR OTHER FAMILY MEMBERS

A consequence of increased life expectancy is that members of at least three generations in a family are likely to be alive, so that a larger portion of middle-aged adults simultaneously has both parents and children. The terms "sandwich generation" and "women in the middle" were coined to describe middle-aged adults "caught" between the needs of their children and those of their parents.[65] To emphasize the severity of this problem, the worst possible cases often are cited — for example, a single, employed mother who has preschool children and a demented mother living with her.[66] Recent research shows that it is unusual for adult children to have very young children and very old parents simultaneously.[67] Knowing that such situations are atypical should not reduce concern for daughters such as the one described above, but information about less dire situations may allay some of the fears of old parents and their offspring.

In the 149 families included in this study, the siblings' children ranged in age from very young to middle-aged. Most were at least teenagers or in their 20s, but in some sibling groups, there was variation among members with respect to presence of dependent children.

In some groups, at least one sibling had no children. Citing this reason, a brother explained why his sister did more for their mother:

My sister doesn't have children, and I feel she assumed this role because she saw that my duties with my growing children were taking a great deal of my time and energy. (*Brother with one sister and one brother*)

Conversely, a brother who had no children explained why his parents spent more time with his brother:

My brother will have my parents out to the house more often. He's [geographically] closer. He has the grandchildren. I don't. They have a fair amount of contact. The grandchildren provide all sorts of emotional support to them. That's what grandchildren are for. (*Brother with one brother*)

A sister who had no children complained about her brother because she felt that his children should be more involved with their grandmother:

I would like more free time to go on vacations. My husband is retired and is not happy about the situation. It would be a real help if only one of the grandchildren came out. (*Sister with one brother*)

Had she children of her own, complaining about her nieces might not have been an option.

Some siblings had very young children, while their nieces and nephews were older:

We're all in touch constantly. Not my brother so much. He's not in the decision-making process so much. He usually waits to hear what we feel and goes along with it. I think it's because he has younger children, and they take a lot of time. (*Sister with two sisters and one brother*)

I'd certainly like to do a little more. With this distance it's kind of hard to do that. And I have young children around. (*Brother with one brother*)

She would probably call my brother if a problem arose. He's closer to her in his work place and also has been sort of a pillar for her. Also, his kids are more grown up. (*Brother with two brothers*)

Both difference in parental status and difference in age of children, then, were cited by the informants as reasons that one sibling did more than another.

In addition to dependent children, some siblings referred to the needs of their own or their siblings' parents-in-law as a reason why someone did less:

My brother has problems with his father-in-law who lives with him; so he can't be doing that much for my dad. (*Sister with one brother*)

I think he is doing what he can. He has a mother-in-law in a nursing home near where he lives. (*Brother with one brother*)

As I've said, one brother is doing less partly because of geographic distance and his own problems. His mother-in-law was sick for a long time and ultimately died. That absorbed his energies. (*Brother with three brothers*)

One brother explained why his sister was doing less than he was:

> My sister's husband had a serious car accident. She has
> not been as available for the past year. (*Brother with*
> *one sister and two brothers*)

Dependent family members were not restricted to children.
Siblings' responsibilities for other family members were not
equivalent.

RELATIVE HEALTH STATUS

With few exceptions the parents in these families were
at least 75 years of age, some in their 90s. Consequently,
some of their children were in late middle- or early-old age.
The older someone is, the more likely she or he is to have
a chronic health condition due to injury or illness. Health
status, then, is an issue not only for old parents but for adult
children as well.

In some groups relative health of sibling-group members
was cited to explain why the division of labor was unequal.
A sister explained why her mother was more likely to ask
her brother for assistance:

> It's up to my mother, but I think she wants my brother
> more. Maybe because of my leg, she wants him to do
> more. I am suffering with leg circulation problems,
> and driving and walking is a slight problem for me.
> (*Sister with one brother*)

Her brother concurred, although he depicted his sister's
health problems as more serious:

> I am more mobile, more willing and more physically
> able. My sister has more physical problems. She's not
> able to walk easily. (*Brother with one sister*)

Other informants also cited health problems as a reason that they or their siblings did less:

> His own personal family situation has been such that he can't do as much. He's on disability, having had heart surgery, and his wife had major surgery in September. His daughter-in-law is having a difficult pregnancy. So his personal situation is what makes a difference. (*Sister with two brothers*)

> One of my brothers has physical problems and can't do as much as the rest of us. (*Brother with three brothers*)

> My sister, even though she's working, has taken over more because of my recent illness. (*Sister with one sister*)

> One sister is not working, but her illness prevents her from doing things that my sister and I do. (*Sister with three sisters and one brother*)

Difference in health status among siblings was used to justify the healthier doing more.

RELATIVE SOCIAL CLASS AND

DISCRETIONARY INCOME

Members of a sibling group have the same social-class background by virtue of being launched by the same parents, but their class standings may diverge thereafter.[68] As adults they are likely to differ to some degree with respect to discretionary income and on the standard components of social class: educational attainment, family income, and occupational prestige.

In the following two families, relative social class or "success" is the issue raised by a brother in each sibling group:

> I have different values from my brothers. They are attorneys and feel different about money and success and lifestyle. That interferes with our working together and liking one another. We had a family reunion last June — sometimes unfinished business from growing up emerges, and then there's some tension around that doesn't get resolved. (*Brother with two brothers*)

> We were really much at odds when we were growing up, and it is pretty much the same today. He is jealous of the fact that I am where I am financially and status-wise, and he is still struggling. He was always against whatever I was for, and that is still in existence today. (*Brother with one brother*)

Others focused on discrepant financial situations:

> I'm 62 and have no retirement. I could get kicked out of this job at any time; it's a possibility. Plus, having six kids does something to one's equity. I'd be less able [than my brothers] to help my mother financially. (*Brother with two brothers*)

> I suppose she might tend to call my brother first. His financial situation has been better up to now. (*Sister with one brother*)

References to difference in financial standing were sometimes disguised. In the following, an employed sister cited her small, two-bedroom apartment as the reason that her mother stayed with her sister when she visited for two months in the summer. Her midlife divorce meant that the sister's lifestyle was very different from hers:

> My sister gives her room and board when she's here. My sister has three empty bedrooms and two empty bathrooms. When my mother stays with me, someone else loses a bedroom. (*Sister with one sister*)

In another family a sister explained why one of her sisters could not do as much as she would have liked: "There isn't anything my sister could do at this point. If she had her own home or was working successfully, she would insist Mother be with her" (*Sister with five sisters and one brother*).

When parents required financial assistance, the issue of disparate financial situations was difficult to sweep under the rug. The decision to place their mother in a nursing home led to an agreement between two sisters about their contributions to the cost. One sister was financially well off, while her sister, who had been divorced in middle age, said that she was working in part to cover the expenses required to visit her children. Their mother was to be placed in a nursing home in the near future. One sister explained how she and her sister would help pay for their mother's care:

> She'll get help from my husband and me and my sister and her husband. When you apply you have to give them information about your financial situation. You sign a paper to guarantee that her costs will be covered. It will be representative — the amount, not the feeling. We sat down and agreed what it will be. (*Sister with one sister*)

In another family one brother, who paid his mother's rent in a retirement community, said: "I support her financially.

My brother is not in a position to contribute financially"
(*Brother with one brother*).

Another consideration was which siblings would benefit
financially when parents died:

> My mother's house will eventually go to my sister;
> so she takes care of major repairs. (*Sister with one
> sister*)

> The house will be mine eventually, and my brothers
> think that's right because I'll have to take care of the
> folks. (*Sister with two brothers*)

In one family the parents had sold their own home to move
into a duplex with their son and his wife. One sister said,
"I don't mean this to sound bad, but my brother wanted a
home and didn't have the money for the down payment." In
the near future her parents and her brother's family were
moving to a new home in a suburb:

> My mother and my sister-in-law didn't get along very
> well. I was surprised that they decided to build the
> house with the in-law suite. My sister-in-law will say,
> "We have the responsibility of your parents," but they
> asked for it. If my parents hadn't sold their house so
> they could buy, they wouldn't have a home. (*Sister with
> one sister and one brother*)

Her sister concurred:

> I feel guilty about not being nearer my mother and not
> visiting them a lot, but then I feel my brother and his
> wife initiated it by moving in together; so they knew
> they would assume more responsibility. (*Sister with
> one sister and one brother*)

Relative financial status entered into the division of family labor in a number of ways, including social class or "success," expendable income and resources with which to provide monetary and other assistance to parents, and how siblings' benefited differently from their parents' assets.

SENIORITY

Throughout their shared lives, siblings stand in relation to one another on the basis of their order of arrival. In same-gender sibling groups, relative age may be more important than in mixed-gender ones simply because gender cannot be used to differentiate the members of the group. Even with this study's two sets of twins, in each family one sibling was older (in two-sibling groups) or oldest (in sibling groups of three or more), and one sibling younger or youngest. Age differences between siblings were mentioned by informants but usually as an explanation for why they "did not work together" when they were children.[69] Referring to their relationships in adulthood, seniority or relative time of arrival, rather than age, was used to explain who did what with and for old parents, although siblings often used "age" inappropriately as a proxy for "seniority."

One brother explained he did more did for his parents than his brother — "because I'm [geographically] closer and I'm the older child" (*Brother with one brother*). Another brother complained that his older brother was getting more information and more credit from their mother:

> I think it's basically that my brother, being older, is the first one to get the information from either Mother or the doctor, as with Dad's illness. I think it's basically because of his age. (*Brother with one brother*)

Two members of a four-member sibling group agreed that the oldest would be called first in an emergency:

> If there's only one party that would be likely to take a lead position, it'd likely be my brother because he's the oldest. (*Brother with three brothers*)

> I would probably be called first since I'm the oldest. I'm the head of the pecking order. (*Brother with three brothers*)

In some siblings' view, having seniority meant added responsibility:

> I think because I'm the older and had a good school record. The oldest takes on the mantle of responsibility. The oldest has a lot of attention. (*Sister with one sister*)

> There's more burden on my sister probably. She cares the most as the oldest. She probably feels the most responsibility. (*Brother with one sister and one brother*)

> When my father left I became the one who assumed the responsibility. I was four years older than my brother, and I think the answer is really, "There is no change [in our relationship]." He's always followed me along, and I ruled the roost. (*Brother with one brother*)

A sister explained why the oldest child in a group of four siblings was the liaison between them and their father:

> My mother always said, "Your sister will be doing this." A lot of the mentality around this time was the "eldest son," but she was the oldest and was capable, and my mother said that she would take over. My father relates

> best to her because she is the eldest. He always related
> based on age. He's the eldest of his family. (*Sister with
> one sister and two brothers*)

Occasionally, being the youngest was seen as a special status:

> She was closer to my folks because she was the baby and
> was with them as they grew a little older. She's closer
> to my parents than my brother or I. She handles them
> very well. (*Sister with one sister and one brother*)

Siblings in these 149 families, however, rarely cited least seniority to explain a sibling's participation in family labor.

There always is one child who arrives first in a sibling group, one who has seniority. Siblings in most cases indicated that age differences were no longer relevant now that all siblings were adults,[70] but seniority was used by some siblings to justify why the older or oldest had specific responsibilities.

Siblings' relative positions on these eight attributes were used to explain who did more and who did less of the family labor of meeting parents' needs. Logically, the smaller the collective differences between or among siblings on these attributes, the more difficult it should have been to justify unequal participation. Whether this logic holds is the subject of Chapter 7. Before turning to that issue, two other factors are addressed: gender differences and the participation of parents in the division of family labor.

CHAPTER FIVE

GENDER DIFFERENCES IN APPROACHES TO MEETING PARENTS' NEEDS

GENDER IS ONE of the relative attributes that siblings used to explain who did what with and for their parents. In mixed-gender sibling groups, it was difficult for respondents to talk about the division of family labor without reference to gender. As was clear in Chapter 3, some tasks were more likely to be performed by either brothers or sisters. Chapter 4 presented evidence that siblings used gender to explain specific and differential involvement in family labor. In this chapter the focus is on differences in how brothers and sisters approached meeting their parents' needs. At issue here is that brothers and sisters had different ideas about how best to meet their parents' needs.[71]

Most research that explores gender differences in the provision of care to old parents simply compares sons to daughters without attending to their status as siblings. Regardless of the way care is measured, daughters, as a category, with few exceptions, are found to provide more services and to spend more time providing them than are sons.[72] There is general agreement that daughters do more than sons for their old parents: "When the parents' need for help progresses to more intense tasks such as daily household chores or personal care, sons abdicate the role."[73]

Some researchers, however, have suggested that the gender difference may be exaggerated because of the specific tasks about which children typically are asked.[74] Helping parents (or anyone else) with bathing, dressing, toileting, getting in/out of bed, getting around inside, and eating are more likely to be done for family members by women than by men in our society, as are shopping, doing laundry, preparing meals, and housework. The only task that men are more likely to perform is financial management.[75] If the list included more tasks associated with the male role, then sons might look better; however, they still would be found wanting, because brothers' contributions are measured by a feminine yardstick.[76] What became clear from listening to the siblings' accounts was that brothers and sisters differed with respect to what they considered the best approach to meeting their parents' needs.[77]

After identifying the key points of difference, a typology of styles of involvement in meeting parents' needs is introduced. This typology was originally developed to describe sibling groups that included at least two sisters, two of whom were interviewed. Analysis of the brothers' interviews, however, suggested that the original typology, while valid, was biased, in that it assumes implicitly that the sisters' approach is better. The value of interviewing brothers about family life, rather than relying solely on their sisters' versions, is evident in this chapter.[78]

How Best to Meet Parents' Needs

When old parents needed assistance, the best way to provide it was not necessarily something on which everyone agreed. The research literature on the division of household labor and child care has focused primarily on how evenly the work is divided, usually by comparing hours devoted to housework and child care. It also provides evidence — although it is somewhat thinner — that husbands and wives rarely agree on such things as how clean the house should be and how much attention a child requires. In other words, which person spends more time is the focus, rather than who decides what should be done.[79] This also applies to the family labor of meeting parents' needs. An underlying assumption in much of the research on parent care is that an appropriate response is inherent in a specific need — that if someone spends eight hours helping a parent, it is because the parent requires eight hours of assistance. In fact, there are many ways to respond to particular needs,[80] and there is likely to be disagreement about which is the best.

The sampling design for this study made it possible to see that what should be done was as important an issue in some of the sibling groups as who should perform a task. Differences of opinion were related to gender. Comparisons among pairs of sisters, pairs of brothers, and sister-brother pairs revealed subtle differences in brothers' and sisters' approaches that have important consequences for how sibling groups divide family labor and, in turn, for the type of support parents are likely to receive from their children. The issues on which different views were held are reported — first from the brothers' perspective, then from the sisters'.

Waiting to be Asked vs. Monitoring

Rather than volunteering their services, brothers expected their parents to ask for assistance. The two mothers described below required transportation:

> We both take her shopping, any place she wants to go. Whoever she can find first is asked to take her. (*Brother with one brother*)

> If she needs to go someplace and she doesn't have transportation, one of us will always take her or arrange for transportation. There's no set schedule. It's as the need arises. (*Brother with two brothers*)

Both brothers indicated that they expected their mothers to let them know when they needed a ride.

Parents also were described by brothers as orchestrating contributions: "She's very smart. She'll piecemeal the work. She'll divide it up, give me something to do, and save something for my brother to do" (*Brother with one brother*). Even during relatively difficult transitions, brothers expected parents to ask for assistance: "When my father died eight years ago, she went on to independent living. I don't think she started leaning on us for more support" (*Brother with one brother*). Because their contact with parents was often on the telephone, nonproximate brothers had to rely on their parents to tell them if they needed assistance. Proximate brothers were in a position to monitor their parents' circumstances. Regardless of how far they lived from their parents, however, brothers viewed their parents (unless they were seen as mentally incompetent) as capable of making decisions about their lives, including how their sons should be involved.

Sisters, too, responded to parents' requests for assistance, but they also indicated that they monitored their parents. They were less inclined to take their parents at their word. A sister who lived with her mother said:

> When I go to work in the morning and my mother seems more depressed, I'll call my sister and tell her to get in touch with Mom. She'll come over, all the way from the West Side, and visit with my mother or take her out. She's very supportive. (*Sister with one sister*)

Rather than relying on her mother to recognize her need for company and to call her daughter, she acted in her mother's stead. She described the period following their father's death five years earlier:

> She felt very lost. Their generation, their social life was their family, and after my father died, she didn't know how to make friends or how to project herself. That's why she's working. She has a social life there as a waitress. This summer I think she's a little better than she had been. Last Sunday we gave a dinner party and it was the first time she's enjoyed doing this since my father died. I think she's finally getting over it; but if you've never made friends in your life, it's hard to start at age 75. (*Sister with one sister*)

The sister had "monitored" the recovery of her mother over the previous five years as she adjusted to widowhood. Similarly, a sister in another family described her widowed father:

> We watch his diet, and he's putting on weight. We tell him he shouldn't have so many sweets. He buys those goodies for himself. We try to get him to watch his health. (*Sister with five sisters*)

Sisters, like brothers, responded to parents' requests but also monitored their parents, gave them advice, and attempted to intervene when they thought it was appropriate.

Adult Child vs. Sibling

A second gender difference in the approach to family labor was that brothers were more likely to view their relationships with their parents as distinct from their relationships with their siblings. While they acknowledged that they were both sons and brothers, they viewed the two relationships as independent, except during a crisis. This is a logical outcome of brothers taking direction from their parents. Because they expected their parents to ask for assistance, there was no reason for them to interact with their siblings *about* their parents.

When discussing routine contact with his mother, one brother said:

> I'll call my mother and ask, "Have you heard from them [brother and wife]?" At times she'll say, "not in a month"; at times it'll be, "yesterday." I think my mother probably has had some dry spells, doesn't hear from either of us. Other times she has feast times, hears from both of us. It's not something we schedule, and maybe we should. We haven't sat down and said, "Call then, so a week doesn't go by. . . . " (*Brother with one brother*)

The same point is emphasized in another brother's description of what occurred when his mother needed help after surgery:

When she had her first hip done, she was in the hospital for ten days. I went and took care of her for about a week when she got out. When she got her second hip done in May, my older brother came up to look after her for a week or so. I was actually surprised he came up the second time to take care of her. I would have; but due to circumstances, there was no way I could. I was surprised he found the time to do that. (*Brother with one brother*)

Thus, the brothers did not routinely discuss with one another what they were doing with and for their parents but acted independently.

Health crises and major transitions in their parents' lives, however, galvanized brothers:

We both talked to the doctor. We made decisions jointly to make sure of what needed to be done to take care of her. I took care of getting her a Lifeline to have some security. The normal things for her well-being we discuss if we feel it's necessary to discuss. (*Brother with one brother*)

Now, when my father was real sick, we all got together and talked about what nursing home he should go into. Three of us, I think, went out and viewed nursing homes together and decided which one [was best]. (*Brother with three brothers*)

When father passed away two years ago, that was the only time I discussed Mother with my brothers, mostly with the one here in town. He and I see each other about once a week and talk about finances. We never discuss what would happen if Mother got sick. If that happens we will take care of it then. (*Brother with two brothers*)

Except when parents had health crises and faced transitions, then, brothers tended not to act as a team but rather to act as sons, each responding directly to parents' requests for assistance.

Sisters were more likely to communicate with their siblings in addition to their parents. They were aware of what both brothers and sisters were doing:

> We don't stand on ceremony in our family. If I can't do something, my sister does it. If she can't, I do it. We are both very flexible. We're both available to help each other or anyone else in the family. I can't provide long-term residence as well as she can, but I can get my mother out of the house on Saturday. That's my contribution to my sister's mental health when my mother is visiting from Florida. It's always been that we help one another, one big family. (*Sister with one sister*)

A sister explained why responsibility for their mother fell more to her than to her sister:

> Because of her work basically. She has problems and crises in her home, too. And when you're financially concerned about money. . . .I try to relieve her, take the pressure off her. And she still has children at home. And she's more sensitive and would get more easily upset. I'd feel it, but I can control myself better. I'm more realistic. (*Sister with one sister*)

In talking about what she did for her parents, this sister talked as much about protecting her sister from additional responsibilities. Another sister described how she and her sister approached doing things for their parents:

> My sister and I don't tell each other what to do. It's just natural. We do what we each do when it's neces-

sary. I think she does more than I do. She does odd little things, the niceties of life. She's a giving person. She sends them clippings or cartoons in the mail. She will send them things on the spur of the moment from stores. My sister will go camping with them, in their own trailer, more often than I will. I'm just always here for Mom and Dad. When my dad wasn't driving for about eight weeks, I did all the driving and took Mom shopping. I will make phone calls for him, when he is looking for items for his trailer. I take my mom Christmas shopping, which is a real bear. My sister has no patience with my mom in the store. Usually when there is a need for something like shopping, they come to me. My sister does the out-of-the-way things that she thinks of while she is out — for example, buying things for them like things for the house. (*Sister with one sister*)

Another sister indicated that she and her sister spoke regularly to one another about their mother. She did not trust their mother to identify her own needs:

My sister and I talk every day. We find Mother colors what she tells us; so we find it best to communicate daily. Absolutely, we discuss her medical problems. You can't go blind into these things. We do talk about it. (*Sister with one sister*)

Unlike brothers, then, when sisters talked about doing things for their parents, they also talked about what they did for their siblings. They viewed themselves as part of a family system in which being a daughter and a sister were interdependent, while brothers viewed their ties to each family member as independent. When crises occurred or family decisions were required because of impending transitions, sisters already were galvanized.

Promoting Independence

vs. Accepting Dependence

When changes in functional health status, marital status, or friendship networks undermined their parents' sense of security or independence, brothers' goal in assisting parents was to make their circumstances once again match their abilities. This sometimes involved more assistance from them, particularly if the time period or task required for extra support was bounded; but if it was not, other sources were tapped. Brothers expected their parents to make changes that would make them self-sufficient again.

A brother whose father recently had been diagnosed as demented, said: "My father always handled financial affairs. I advised my mother to take control of the situation, and now I've suggested a financial planner" (*Brother with one brother*). If she took his advice, his mother would remain independent of him. A brother described the circumstances surrounding his mother's recent move from Cleveland, where her more proximate son had been a four-hour drive away:

> When Mother lived in Cleveland, she had an emergency call button that she had to push twice a day that went to the police department. She was very close to her church, two blocks away. There were people there who knew her well and could help her. If there was a problem in the evening, the pastor lived nearby. She had resources she could draw on — for example, the maintenance man at church. She had very close contact with those people. She had a housekeeper who came once a week.

She also had friends whom she transported in her car. These circumstances made it feasible for her to continue safely to live alone, even though she had numerous health problems. Shortly before his interview, she had moved to a retirement community approximately an hour's drive from one of her two sons and a ten-minute drive from the recent widow of her third son:

> Besides the unsteadiness on her feet, there are some other things that bother her. She has had some problems with her feet. She also has some problem with her heart — sort of an arrhythmia. The doctor has given her medication for it that has contributed to the unsteadiness. She has also had a balance problem. She was living alone in a large house that had three floors. It was getting to be a rather heavy job taking care of it. She had a big yard with a lot of huge trees. In the fall there were a lot of leaves to get up. In the wintertime there was the ice and snow problem. Last winter she fell three times in the house. She was not hurt, but it alarmed her to an extent. I had an uncle, my father's brother-in-law, who died a year and a half ago, the last immediate family in the Cleveland area. My mother has no brothers or sisters left in the Cleveland area. Of the three sons, one died a year ago. That's what brought the decision to move: no family there and fear of falling or getting sick in the house with no one there. It was a very difficult decision for her to make. (*Brother with one brother*)

This mother, then, whose situation in a single-family home became increasingly precarious, made the decision to move to a more sheltered setting and, as a consequence, remained self-sufficient. Her sons both facilitated and approved of her move.

A brother in another family began his description of who did what for his widowed mother by saying: "Well, there are no contributions. She's been fairly independent up until now." Since his mother had broken her hip in a one-car accident a year earlier, she had not been able to drive: "It really limited her ability to be mobile. It changed her lifestyle immensely." Late in the interview he said that his mother had stayed with him and his wife for three weeks after her accident and that she had had "the visiting nurse, those auxiliary services." He described what he currently did for his mother, who again was living in her single-family home forty minutes away:

> The day-to-day things of looking after her I do. I've done a lot of yard work for her, but I'm really trying to encourage her to run her own life. I try to encourage her to be more active, less dependent than she already is. I go there two or three times a week. I try to avoid a regular calling schedule. I don't want to get into that. I call about every other day. There's a retarded man in the neighborhood who does her lawn work. I used to do it all. For her best interests, we make her as independent as possible. My wife and I are willing to help her with anything she can't do. For financial things she's independent. She basically handles her financial affairs on her own. Complicated bills I help her with, Medicare. I try to get her to handle things. For example, the state is trying to pull her license. They did pull it. I let her call first. We didn't get an acceptable answer, so I called to see what could be done to get her license. (*Brother with one brother*)

This brother's contributions, then, were intended to reestablish his 85-year-old mother's independence.

Brothers were frustrated when parents would not adapt to changed circumstances. A pair of brothers despaired that their parents would ever adjust to retirement. One said:

> They are both basically in good health. They are affluent. They are basically unhappy, not with each

other, but they are not happy to be old. They are both depressed. That is their primary problem. My father requires more activity than he can find. They drink too much in trying to deal with this problem. They are basically lonely and bored. They have lost all of the *joie de vivre* and lack energy and initiative to do anything. (*Brother with one brother*)

He said that to fix this situation, he and his wife had "encouraged them to get therapy." Although his parents followed the advice, neither went for long. At the time of the interview, he said that he and his brother were "not angry with them anymore, although we have lost respect for them." Nevertheless, both brothers continued to spend time with their parents regularly, but one said: "We see them as a filial obligation. Sometimes we have a good time." These brothers said that they discussed their parents' situation frequently. Brothers whose parents' situations were unstable were in more frequent contact with one another.

Throughout the interviews brothers described support networks that contributed to their parents continued independence. The mother described above, who moved from Cleveland, had an extensive network. One nonproximate brother said that if his parents had needs, "they are being met by a cast of thousands." He doubted that his brother who lived near his parents would be called first in an emergency, because his parents had friends that were his age in the immediate neighborhood. Another pair of brothers, neither living in the same town as their widowed mother, described an extensive network that included their mother's two sisters and a sister-in-law, as well as many friends whom she had known since high school. A widowed mother who had had a stroke that "affected her mobility slightly" paid the custodian in her condominium building a monthly fee to drive her in her car. Both proximate brothers saw this as an acceptable solution to her transportation needs, although they also provided transportation. The size of her friendship network was emphasized by one brother, who said: "She has so many people paying attention to her, sometimes you have to call her three or four times. You think something's wrong, and she's just out" (*Brother with two brothers*).

In its many forms, congregate housing for the elderly functions as a support network. One pair of brothers described their parents' moves — first into an apartment, then to an apartment for senior citizens, and most recently to an assisted-living apartment. Except during the moves, the brothers' contributions remained approximately the same, because each residential move increased the resources available to their parents. These moves made it possible for the brothers to continue to describe their parents as self-sufficient.

One brother, whose 86-year-old father lived in a retirement community, said:

> I think that's one of the most important things an older parent can do for his adult children — stay as independent as possible in a place where they're taken care of — pay for their own care and yet be close enough where he can see his family. And that way no one has to feel guilty or mad that someone isn't doing something. (*Brother with one brother*)

The two brothers lived near their father. They both saw him almost weekly at lunch, invited him to their homes regularly, and one saw him at church once a week. They knew someone on the staff of the retirement community who would get in touch with them if there were a problem. One brother said: "We really don't do anything for him, as far as I'm concerned. We offer a lot, but he doesn't accept. He wants to do it all himself as long as he can." The brothers, then, saw this situation as ideal. Such settings insured that parents remained self-sufficient.

Throughout these interviews, then, there is a great deal of evidence that it was not the brothers alone but a network — informal, formal, or a combination — that the brothers identified as contributing to their parents' independence. Brothers did not expect to be the sole source of support for their parents. One brother said: "We do what we're capable of doing. I think it's a terrible mistake to do something you're not capable of because, then, you wind up feeling frustrated instead of useful" (*Brother with one brother*).

In contrast to brothers, sisters responded to changes in their parents' functional health status, marital status, or friendship networks, which undermined their parents' independence, by providing services, even while taking care to preserve their parents' autonomy. Rather than expecting their parents to change residence or to use formal services to reestablish independence, they were more likely to provide services themselves and become more involved in their parents' lives. Even when formal services were used, they tended to monitor them closely.

When asked what would happen to her relationship with her father if her mother were to die, a sister said, "I'd want to go there and see he's eating right, wash his clothes, clean his house, take over the wifely duties" (*Sister with one sister*). A sister described her 97-year-old mother, who lived in a retirement hotel and whose health status would be rated by most measures as very poor:

> In the last year, healthwise, she's hard of hearing and she's much worse. She can't hear over the telephone. She does wear a hearing aid, but it doesn't help much. She doesn't get out unless we take her. She has angina.

> She's a little afraid to go, even in her building. She takes medication for angina regularly. She doesn't get out of her apartment for weeks on end unless we take her. She gets around very well in the apartment. My sister and I get her groceries. She's a little afraid of going out in the last few years. (*Sister with one sister and two brothers*)

Her sister's assessment was similar:

> She's very independent in her own apartment. She's had angina for forty to fifty years. She takes many pills and knows every one. She checks to be sure they are right. We never have to worry about that. She has good sense. She is a *grande dame* in a sense. She creates that respect in us. She's a very bright woman and knows what she's doing. She has a marvelous sense of humor. Loneliness is the biggest problem. She craves company. She has high blood pressure, takes pills for that. She had a mastectomy two years ago. She had cataracts eight years ago. She had gall bladder surgery three or four years ago. She took those so well. She doesn't go under her own steam. She says she can't because her heart acts up, but it's also because she's frightened. So she won't do that much. We take her out, not as much as we used to. Her apartment is far from the elevator and so we wheel her to the car and then she walks a little. It's a chore to take her out now. She is very deaf. I have to find different ways to say the same thing so that she'll hear one word and get the gist of it. (*Sister with one sister and two brothers*)

The sisters responded to their mothers' increased isolation by visiting more often and running more errands for her, so that she could continue to live in her apartment. The two sisters, one brother, and another "unreliable" brother, were paying her rent because she had "run out of money" approximately four years earlier. Rather than encourage their mother to move to a more protected environment (in order to hold constant their contributions to her), the sisters responded by increasing the amount of time they spent thinking about her and doing things for her, including making financial contributions.

Sisters were frustrated not with recalcitrant parents but with their inability to put together an adequate support network. One sister described her mother: "Manic-depression was what happened over night. She was very self-sufficient up to the age of 80." Her mother lived in a senior-citizens housing complex, but she and her sister had arranged for someone to be with their mother 24 hours a day because of their fear that she might commit suicide. Despite the presence of the "nurses," they were in regular contact with their mother and with the women who watched her:

> I do the shopping, medical, clothes. My sister may fill in once in a while. I do the banking. Anything monetary I take care of. She and I were dividing up Sundays because the nurse takes a day off. We go there and get Mom. This last year she was so down and we're getting weary of listening to her. And she is particularly different to us than she is to the nurse. It got to where we split the day. She'll complain she can't walk, but she's okay. Her depression is contagious. I felt bad for my sister, because she works and she didn't have even the one day free. In April we talked about getting someone to help stay with her that one day. We found someone, and Mother seemed to like her. But now that girl may leave. I had to take care of it because my sister was out of town. I phone every morning and seldom at night because that's a good time for my sister to call. My sister may call at lunch, too. Mother does go to all building activities. She's taken by the nurse. My sister may talk to the nurse to see how Mom is, so we know what's happening. (*Sister with one sister*)

Even though the sisters had engaged others to attend to their mother, they continued to monitor her situation and to remain very actively involved in her daily life.

Two sisters were providing help to their indomitable mother, who had been living with one of them for a year:

> After her hospitalization and her awful health deterioration resulting from it, she moved to my sister's so someone could take care of her, and we sold her house. It's a sort of temporary arrangement until we settle on something more permanent and maybe she'll be better able to care for herself. My mother has to have at least four doctors' appointments a week, because of severe ulcerated feet, and be bandaged four times a day. She requires a lot of time and attention. (*Sister with one sister*)

They did not hurry their mother into a more protected setting to reestablish her independence from them. Instead, the two sisters assembled a network comprising family members to meet her needs:

> This summer we have to plan because she has to see doctors four times a week, two each week. Then also, we use our children for a lot of Grandma's errands. I have a son and daughter at home, and my sister has a daughter, and they do a lot of the tasks. We look at our schedules and just fit ourselves in conveniently. During the school year, I do all the doctor appointments, hair dressers, church activities, etc. But now my sister tries to do as much as she can to compensate for my winter running. (*Sister with one sister*)

In another family a sister lived next door to her father who shared a two-family home with her sister:

He's happy and his health is very good. He even plays golf — nine holes of it. He's still able to drive his car and likes to go to get his lunch at a drive-in. He gets his own breakfast and can cook for himself. He takes the dog out and looks forward to us coming home. My sister cooks for him at night. My mother did everything for him. He doesn't even make his bed. I help with house cleaning and help my sister, and my other sister helps. We all talk to him about pleasant things, try to keep him cheerful. And I send my husband over to him when he wants to talk to a man. (*Sister with five sisters*)

Rather than expecting their parents to arrange their own networks or assembling networks so that their parents could once again be independent of them, sisters became increasingly involved in their parents' lives and expected their parents to depend on them.

In summary, sisters and brothers differed in their approach to meeting their parents' needs. Brothers responded to parents' requests for assistance, while sisters not only responded to requests but also monitored their parents and offered unsolicited services and advice. Brothers made contributions as sons to their parents. Sisters expected to share responsibility with their brothers and sisters and saw their own contributions to their parents in relation to their siblings', acting not only as daughters but also as sisters. The brothers' aim in providing assistance was to enable their parents to reestablish self-sufficiency. They saw as legitimate their parents' use of both formal and informal support networks to accomplish this goal. Parents who refused to act to regain self-sufficiency frustrated brothers. On the other hand, as their parents became more needy, sisters responded by increasing services, accepting increased dependence on them as appropriate. They saw the problem as

finding enough time and appropriate services to supplement
their own contributions to their parents.

PARTICIPATION STYLES

These gender differences in approaches to meeting parents' needs are related to participation styles identified in an
early paper[81] that focused only on the fifty sibling groups that
each included at least two sisters. Based on sisters' perceptions of the predictability and availability of their siblings,
five participation styles were identified to describe how siblings were involved in meeting their parents' needs. They
are presented here, first, as initially formulated. Then, their
applicability to sibling groups in which there was only one
or no sisters is evaluated.

Routine participation described siblings whose regular
assistance to elderly parents was incorporated into their ongoing activities. Because parents varied with respect to what
was needed, routine involvement included a wide range of
activities: household chores ("I do Mom's cleaning, dusting,
vacuuming, and laundry"); "checking" ("I call my mother
twice every day"); providing outings ("Every Tuesday I take
Mother shopping for the day"); running errands ("I've always done Mother's grocery shopping"); managing finances
("I pay all of Mother's bills"); and visiting ("Tuesday and
Saturday afternoons I spend visiting her").

A second style was being a *back-up*. Some siblings were
not routinely involved in providing emotional support or
concrete services but could be counted on when siblings
who were engaged in routine activities asked them to help.
For example, one sister explained, "I do what my sisters
instruct me to do." There was apparently no doubt that she
would respond to her sisters' instructions, but she did not

initiate involvement. Siblings who used this style could be counted on to do whatever they were asked to do, but they were expected to be available primarily when siblings who were routinely involved decided that they were needed.

Circumscribed was a style of participation that was highly predictable but bounded. Siblings who adopted this style could be counted on to help, but there were clear limits to what they were called upon to do. One sister said of her brother, "He gives a routine, once-a-week call." This call was important to their parent, and her brother could be relied upon to make it, but he apparently was not available or expected to increase the scope of his participation in the provision of care to their mother. A brother who was a physician was relied upon for medical advice or assistance when it was needed, but he was not expected by his sisters to assume any other responsibility.

In contrast to the predictable nature of the contributions associated with the preceding styles, the *sporadic* style was used to describe siblings who provided services or interacted with their parents at their own convenience. One sister said, "We invite Mom to go along when we take trips." Another said, "My brother does come in when he feels like it to take Mother out on Sundays, but it's not a scheduled thing." Even though sporadic involvement was seen as unreliable, it was recognized as valuable to the parent. When parents were perceived to have increased need for services, however, siblings who continued to use this style apparently did not acknowledge that coordinated efforts might meet those needs more effectively. Sisters did not necessarily view this as a problem. One sister said about one of her four sisters, "Whatever she does is okay with us."

The last style was *dissociation*. Siblings who used this style were predictable in that they could not be counted on for assistance. In one family of three sisters, the two younger ones were involved routinely in helping their mother, while one said that their older sister "is not included in our discussions or dealings with my mother. She doesn't do anything." In some families these siblings apparently had dissociated themselves from the entire family, but this was not always the case. Early in his life the brother in one family had broken off contact with the mother but not with his sisters. His sister explained: "My brother has no interest at all and does not care about my mother to any extent. In the few times he comes in from out of town, we deliberately don't discuss Mother with him."

This typology was developed from interviews with pairs of sisters who, in most cases, described their brothers' participation in meeting their parents' needs as circumscribed or sporadic. This pattern matched previous research findings that daughters, not sons, were "primary caregivers" to old parents. Subsequently, however, brothers in an additional ninety-nine families were interviewed: fifty in lone-sister and ninety-eight in brothers-only sibling groups. Their approach to meeting their parents needs, as described above, did not negate the typology constructed for sibling groups comprising at least two sisters but made clear the pejorative nature of the labels *circumscribed* and *sporadic*. Essentially, the four types (excluding *dissociation*) are understood better as capturing the different approaches of sisters and brothers to meeting their parents' needs.

Brothers may have been described as participating in *what appeared to their sisters* to be *circumscribed* and *sporadic* ways because they were responding directly to their parents' requests for assistance, bypassing their sisters. Furthermore, because they responded to their parents exclusively as sons, keeping separate and distinct their role as brother, they did not talk to their sisters about their parents. This prevented their participating as *back-up*. For siblings to occupy *routine* and *back-up* roles, they must communicate with one another and they must view themselves as assisting their siblings as well as their parents. Brothers who viewed themselves exclusively as sons were precluded from seeing themselves as back-up to their siblings. To label brothers' participation as "circumscribed" or "sporadic," however, captures the perceptions of sisters rather than those of brothers. "Obedient" better captures brothers' willingness to respond to their parents' requests.

How Approach Accounts for

Brothers' Poor Reputation[82]

Gendered approaches to parent care may provide the "theory" to explain the "fact" that daughters are more involved in parent care than sons.[83] They also explain the finding that brothers who have sisters are generally more involved with their parents than are brothers who have brothers,[84] and why sisters with brothers feel more burdened that sisters with sisters.[85] How the gendered approaches identified here can account for each of these findings is discussed in turn.

Brothers Do Less than Sisters

Although there is a growing interest in how men care[86] and the conditions under which they provide care,[87] no one has argued that sons provide more care than daughters.[88] One consistent finding, for example, is that daughters interact with their parents on the telephone more often than sons.[89] In order to monitor their parents, daughters must check on them. Responding primarily to requests, as sons are more likely to do, requires contact only when a need arises and, as a consequence, will occur less frequently. Hence, brothers are less likely to be in contact with their parents as often as sisters are. Likewise, accepting a parent's dependence leads to more interaction than encouraging a parent to remain self-sufficient. This would explain the finding that sons are more likely than daughters to "drop out" as parents' needs increase[90] or to be "case managers" rather than provide hands-on care.

Enacting these approaches to "best practice" in a group of siblings, depending on its gender composition and other factors, may further reduce brothers' involvement. Gender differences in what is considered the appropriate way to assist older parents mean that brothers and sisters are unlikely to agree on solutions to their parents' problems or even that their parents have problems. In a contest between sisters and brothers over whose approach should be implemented, sisters have the advantage, although the word "advantage" may be a poor choice to describe their situation. Winning the dispute over what constitutes "best practice" means that sisters will take on more responsibility.

When it comes to "doing family," women know the standard, in this case, for what constitutes *appropriate* care for parents. Sisters, then, have no reason to listen to brothers who have different ideas about how best to meet their parents' needs. According to one sister: "Daughters end up with the mothers, not the boys. We would call my brother after the fact, but never ask his opinion" (*Sister with one sister and one brother*). After all, sisters know best. In sisters' view, brothers should recognize their authority and act accordingly, by following their example and injunctions and doing "what needs to be done."

Sisters are likely to win the contest with their brothers for another reason: they want to do *more* for their parents, while brothers want to do *less.* This means that when sisters institute their own plans, their brothers are precluded from implementing their ideas. A sister who is willing to take her lonely, frail mother into her household, for example, prevents her brother from helping his mother move to an assisted-living apartment where she would be less dependent on her children.

Sisters Increase Brothers' Participation

Whether brothers have sisters or have brothers affects their participation in parent care. Brothers who have sisters must deal with someone who expects them to behave *familially* rather than *filially.* Brothers may not live up to their sisters' expectations; but if brothers wish to remain on good terms with a sister, there is some pressure to comply with her approach. This would explain the consistent findings that brothers who have at least one sister report themselves and are reported by parents to do more with and for their parents than do brothers who have only brothers. Brothers who have sisters are drawn into sisters' ideas of "best practice" and, as a consequence, participate in ways that they might forgo if left to implement their own approach.

Brothers who only have brothers are likely to share an approach. As a son, each brother is able to do for his parents what he views is required. Each responds to his parents' requests independently. No attempt is made to coordinate actions unless there is a crisis, in which case brothers come together to institute a plan on which it is relatively easy to agree, because their ideas about what is appropriate are likely to be quite similar. Because brothers opt to maintain their parents' independence rather than encourage dependence, they do less for their parents than sisters do. This is captured in the research literature by the term "case management," something brothers are reputed to do more often than sisters, who opt for providing care themselves. In addition, for brothers to view themselves as "caregivers" is a sign that they have failed to reach their goal of their parents being self-sufficient. In fact, brothers tend to downplay what they do for their parents, describing their contributions as "little" and of little consequence even though, from an objective standpoint, what they do for them is quite significant.[91]

Sisters Burdened with Brothers

Because they have different approaches to "best practice," brothers and sisters are more likely than same-gender siblings to have difficulty agreeing about the best approach. This accounts for the findings that sisters who have at least one brother report significantly higher levels of burden and stress that those who have no brothers. In addition to solving a parent's problems, sisters may also be dealing with brothers who do not support their approach. Essentially, sisters' complaints are that their brothers see their responsibility as filial not as familial.[92] For a brother to participate as his sister instructs, he would need to see himself not only as a son but also as a brother, to allow his ties to his parents to be mediated by his sister.

Most of the data in this chapter come from members of sibling groups comprising only brothers or ones in which there were at least two sisters. That sisters and brothers have different approaches is clearest in these families because there is less conflict over the *content* of family labor. For the most part, brothers agreed with one another about the appropriate approach to meeting their parents' needs, as did sisters. Brothers without sisters had no need to defend themselves from their sisters' accusations. In mixed-gender sibling groups, however, there was more tension. This issue is broached in Chapter 7, where more is said about "burdened sisters." Before turning to family conflict, however, this book addresses parents' participation in the division of family labor.

CHAPTER SIX

INCLUDING PARENTS

As in most research on "primary caregivers," parents in this study did not speak for themselves but were cast in the role of recipient of services. Information about them and their situations was provided by their offspring, who were asked to talk about the division of family labor between or among siblings. Two features of the research design, however, made it difficult to confine the parents solely to this status.

First, by using parent's age rather than functional health status as one criterion for choosing respondents, parents in a wide variety of situations were included. Caregiver studies often focus exclusively on adult children whose parents have Alzheimer's disease or other cognitive impairments, conditions that preclude easy or meaningful communication between an old parent and her or his children. Treating these parents primarily as care recipients seems justified. Findings about the division of family labor in such families, however, are unlikely to apply to children whose parents are able to participate in their care arrangements. Recall from Chapter 2 that only some of the parents implicated in this research were cognitively impaired, while others were described by their children as extremely capable despite their advanced years. The majority of parents were somewhere in-between — that is, in control but dependent to some degree on others to help them maintain their self-sufficiency. Some parents had experienced episodes during which they needed a great deal of help but from which they emerged at approximately the former level of control of their everyday lives. Unlike persons suffering from Alzheimer's disease, they were not on a downward trajectory from which there was no hope of either recovering or leveling off. Although death, of course, was inevitable and, given their advanced ages, imminent, the time preceding it would not necessarily be marked by dementia or extreme dependency.

A second feature of the research design, which made it difficult to ignore that parents were active participants in older family life, was that the siblings were asked to talk about their interactions with their parents, rather than respond to fixed-choice questions. Siblings' descriptions and explanations underscored that their parents were active participants rather than simply recipients. Beginning in the 1980s, when "caregiving" and "caregiver burden" became dominant issues in research on older families,[93] old parents were deprived of voice and were "objectified." Although old parents did not speak for themselves in these 149 families, the siblings made it clear that their parents had a voice in whether and how services were provided to them.[94]

According to the siblings, then, what part did their parents play in the division of family labor? To address this question, two types of data were gleaned from the interviews. One is siblings' descriptions of their parents' involvement in how their needs were met. Parents were not depicted as passive but often as active resisters to advice and arrangements made by their children. Second, even when they required a great deal of assistance, parents rarely depended solely on their children. In the previous chapter the point was made that brothers saw as appropriate a network of support for their parents; sisters, too, mentioned others who were involved with their parents, even though they were less likely to rely on them. That other persons were described by the siblings as significant to their parents challenges the implicit assumption that old parents are socially isolated and dependent exclusively on their children.

THE PARTICIPATION OF PARENTS
IN OLDER FAMILIES

As long as parents were cognitively intact and, in some families, even when they were not,[95] they were described by the siblings as very much in charge of what their children did for them. This was difficult to ignore in spite of the fact that the research design encouraged siblings to describe their parents exclusively as recipients or objects of care. There is much evidence in the previous chapters that parents continued to be active members of their families.[96] Here this argument is made explicitly.

Directing Delivery of Services

Apparently some parents orchestrated how their children met their needs. Siblings said that their parents designated who would assist them with what. A sister described her 80-year-old mother, weakened by a stroke and incontinent, who lived by herself in the home in which she had grown old: "She makes a list of what she wants us to do. You check them off the list and then you sit and talk" (*Sister with one sister and one brother).* Another sister described how the family had dealt with her 87-year-old mother's mental deterioration:

> When Mother's illness started when she was about 80, my father said, "We have to do something." Mother wrote all the checks and banking. Father said to us, "You and your sister have to handle funds. Get a lawyer." And the decision was made for me to handle it. The three of us agreed on the decision, and mother went along. (*Sister with one sister*)

A brother seemed puzzled by the interviewer's question of why he and not either of his brothers recently had assisted his mother:

> I think if she'd ask any one of us to help her move into her new apartment, any one of us would. It's just that she asked one of us. It's not that one of us would help and two of us wouldn't. (*Brother with two brothers*)

Each of the siblings in the following families made it clear that parents' wishes and decisions guided their contributions:

> If a problem arose, she would call my older brothers first because my father wanted them to take over for him. My mother tries to divide the tasks. She doesn't want to be a burden to one particular child and so asks something of each one. (*Sister with five brothers*)

> Mother is the decision-maker still. No one does any organizing of contributions. As long as she is still able, Mother is definitely head of the family. (*Brother with one brother*)

> When my parents moved to Cleveland, they decided to
> move to the East Side rather than the West Side where
> I live, because my brother lives on the East Side and is
> more available and medical facilities are better on the
> East Side. (*Sister with one brother*)

> In the case of my father, if he would have a problem, he
> would call my brother. If my dad thought my mother
> was having a problem, he would call me. If my mother
> needed help with anything, she would call me. (*Sister
> with two brothers*)

> My father would never let my younger sisters take
> him to the doctor. (*Sister with two sisters and one
> brother*)

Throughout the interviews, then, siblings routinely indicated that their parents decided who did what with and
for them. This is not surprising for brothers, who acted as
obedient sons; but sisters also indicated that what services
they provided and how was not a decision that was theirs
alone to make, but one their parents either made alone or
in consultation.

Resisting Assistance

Siblings said that when they tried to assist their parents,
they were sometimes rebuffed. Some parents were extremely
protective of their independence. One sister, whose father
was in Florida for the winter, said: "The other day my father
called about a doctor's bill. I said I'd call the doctor. He was
furious" (*Sister with one brother*). Her brother's assessment
was similar: "You've got to understand: my father demands

a hands-off attitude on his life. My father will not allow us to take part in his life very much" (*Brother with one sister*). One brother explained:

> My mother is the kind of person who doesn't like meddling. She doesn't see herself as a frail individual, and she's not. My brother and I treat her as a normal individual who happens to be 79-years-old. If you started calling her and asking her how she was, she'd say, "Am I supposed to be sick?" (*Brother with one brother*)

Parents also were described as rejecting siblings' solutions for situations that parents did not see as problematic:

> We told my mother that she should go out, but she wouldn't listen. We arranged for help to stay with Dad so she could go out, but she sat there with the help. (*Brother with one brother*)

> I've arranged meals-on-wheels for them twice, but they sent them away. They said they can't afford it, but I think Daddy doesn't want to admit to not being able to care for themselves. (*Sister with one sister*)

One brother said: "We had a helper for my mother, but she wouldn't let her in. She said, 'What do I need it for?'" (*Brother with one sister*). His sister's assessment of their 87-year-old mother was: "To this point she's strong willed. She's not having anybody tell her what to do" (*Sister with one brother*).

Siblings also indicated that they disagreed with their parents' decisions about medical procedures:

> As far as the prostate, we almost had him in for an operation, but at the last minute he bowed out. He's afraid of hospitals and doctors. I think he went in before for something for his prostate — a biopsy, I think.

I think he remembers the pain, so he doesn't want to go under the knife. The problem is bladder leakage — it's embarrassing, but he'd rather be embarrassed than go under the knife. I'm just the opposite — I'd rather go under the knife and get it over with. He's independent, and he makes the decisions. We try to persuade him; we discuss it with him. When he's made up his mind, that's it. We don't try to strongly criticize him. We do discuss it with him, but he's got the final word. We came to the conclusion that he's gonna do what he wants to do. Each, in our own way, tries. We all know he's independent. (*Brother with one sister and two brothers*)

She just had cataract surgery on one eye a few weeks ago. My wife tried to counsel her out of it, but it went okay. (*Brother with two brothers*)

That the mother in this family (described earlier in Chapter 2 as "dependent") was able to prevail seems remarkable, because she was the recipient of an exceptional amount of care supervised by her daughter-in-law. As dependent as she was, her decision was respected by her son and his wife.

Other siblings were unable to dissuade their parents from their choice of residence:

The only problem I feel we got, or point of difference, is where they live; and I can't budge them, so I lay off. It's an area where I grew up, and it's changed. I feel it's not safe for people their age. (*Brother with one brother*)

Parents also were described as resisting passively. Sometimes parents agreed when children gave advice, but time revealed that they were just being polite:

I told her we'd get her to the doctor. Before we left she promised she would, but she hasn't gone to this day.

She'll yes you to death, but she'll do what she wants to do. She's a real stubborn person. (*Sister with one sister*)

They will listen to us tell them about services but not do anything about it. They don't follow through. (*Brother with one brother*)

A brother described his mother's response when someone fixed something that others saw as a problem:

My mother has loose throw rugs around, and all the family has preached to her to get them out because it's risky for her. One granddaughter scooped them up and put them in the basement, and Mother brought them back up. (*Sister with two brothers*)

This direct approach to convince her that throw rugs were a hazard was unsuccessful.

Parents, then, were described by the siblings as refusing their advice and assistance both directly and by passively resisting. Even very dependent parents were described as being able to prevail over the wishes of their children.

Withholding Information

When primary caregivers to frail parents serve as respondents for research on parent care, an implicit assumption is that they know enough about their parents to describe them and their situations accurately. A prerequisite to an adult child's providing a service to a parent is knowledge that the parent needs it. Children who do not live near their parents are especially vulnerable to being kept in the dark, because they have little choice but to rely on their parents or others to tell them if there are problems.

Some parents apparently did not tell their children when they had problems. Siblings sometimes said that parents withheld information from them. They reported being informed after the fact that their parents had had a problem, when it was too late for them to provide assistance:

> A year and a half ago, she fell and broke her pelvis. That set her back. She went to the hospital and never told us she was in the hospital until the next day, although she spoke with me that evening. (*Sister with one sister*)

> She gets to the phone if it rings and makes out that nothing is wrong, and people believe it. If she gets sick enough, she'll get someone to get her to the doctor. We hear about it afterwards. (*Sister with two sisters*)

> Mother had cataract surgery alone last year when my brother was visiting me in Arizona. She didn't even tell us she was doing it until she talked to us after the surgery was over. (*Sister with one brother*)

> As I alluded to before, our family keeps private things private. For example, four or five years ago I called her and asked, "How are you?" She said, "I just got out of the hospital." I didn't even know she was in. (*Brother with one brother*)

Parents sometimes announced their plans after making arrangements so that any advice their children might have given was "too late":

> On her recent trip to California, my mother made the plans and informed my sister and me. We would have preferred that she not go. She's too old to travel alone. Her health problems are worrisome. (*Sister with one sister*)

The degree to which parents withheld information from their children was impossible to know. Very few siblings claimed not to know their parent's situation, but there was some evidence that siblings might know less than they supposed. Many respondents, for example, expressed concern about their parents' driving skills. They often said that their parents no longer drove at night, adding something similar to what one sister said, "but she's never had an accident or anything." How well informed were these assertions? Siblings were confident that they knew enough: "My mother is fairly reticent. She doesn't complain. I have to sometimes "drag" things out of her. But she does discuss real problems" (*Brother with one sister*). What constituted a "real" problem was left to his mother. Sisters who monitored their parents may have been less in the dark than were "obedient" sons, but whether they were totally in the light was questionable.

Sibling respondents could not tell things about their parents that they did not know. Their parents chose what to tell them and what to keep to themselves. In families in which children were antagonistic toward, jealous of, or competitive with one another, some parents may have been very careful with information to avoid causing additional strain. Parents, of course, also may have reported misinformation that caused sibling conflict.

Siblings' Responses

as Evidence of Parents' Control

That siblings reported resorting to manipulation or subterfuge with their parents in attempts to produce desired outcomes also indicates the degree to which parents controlled the situation. One brother who was concerned about his parents' safety said:

> Three years ago they were using a kerosene heater in the middle of the living room. They thought they were saving tremendously on fuel. My wife and I were successful in pointing out to them, when we went there to paint, the damage to the walls and ceilings. We couldn't get across that it was potentially dangerous. But when we prepared the walls for painting, pulled everything away from them, and they saw the difference, that made an impact. (*Brother with two brothers*)

This brother used providing assistance that his parents accepted as a means for a change he wanted them to make. A sister explained that her mother, who was confined to bed, did not like the food that her father was cooking and wanted some household help:

> We all decided it was important, so we talked to Dad. We got some help in. Mom asked us to talk to Dad. Dad could not stand the help around, so he got rid of her, but now he cooks better. (*Sister with four brothers*)

The siblings were able to respond successfully to one of their mother's concerns by ostensibly dealing with another.

Sometimes siblings indicated that they were involved in their parents' lives in ways that their parents did not know. A brother told the interviewer that he had not discussed his mother's medical problems with her: "I didn't talk to her about her anemia because I didn't tell her that I called her doctor" (*Brother with two brothers*). Unhappy with the way his mother was managing her portfolio, another brother said:

> She won't listen to us. Only since I got my own financial advisor to contact her lawyer and trust officer [have they] started to be able to make some changes in how her property's handled. I have made some progress by having our message come through people in Cleveland, through other mouths. She'll listen to them, but not to us. (*Brother with one brother*)

Siblings who worked behind the scenes to influence outcomes provide evidence that parents were in control of their own lives.

By using such words as "allow" or "let," some siblings implied that they controlled their parents' lives. A sister described tension within the family over whose will should prevail:

> She's having a rough time living alone, but she won't let us talk her into other arrangements. She manages her own household, and we help with big things. But she doesn't want anyone around to help. We have tried to, but she gets very upset. She wants to do it her way, and she says she'll do it better next time. She won't listen to any change concerning the house and gets angry. She gets up and walks out of the room. We took her to see a retirement home, and she said it'd be just like living in prison to be there. She didn't like it. We took her to another one, and she wouldn't even get out of the car to look. She's still my mother, and we let her have her say. My brother-in-law is a little harder with her. Everyone feels we're a little too soft with her. (*Sister with one sister*)

The mother was "allowed" by the sisters to stay in her own home. Another sister used similar language to indicate that her father made decisions about his life:

My sister allows him to make decisions. My sister and
I discussed recently that he needs a new refrigerator.
I said, "Let's just get it." She said, "No, we should let
him make the decision." But he doesn't like to spend
money. Father's roof was bowing. My sister asked us
to come out and see if anything needed to be done.
We felt it should be done, but he didn't. We weren't
comfortable with it, but he said, "No." (*Sister with one
sister and two brothers*)

Another sister said, "The philosophy is to allow them as
much independence as possible" (*Sister with one sister*).
Throughout the interviews there was clear evidence that
parents were very much in charge of how services were
delivered to them, so that just who was allowing whom to
do what was often not as transparently obvious as it was
presented to be.

When adult children told of situations in which they successfully overrode their parents' wishes, they tended to be
times when the parents literally could not resist:

When she was lying in bed at the hospital, my sister
and I went in to see her and told her she could either
kick the bucket or put the pacemaker in. It took a lot
of convincing. It was against her religion. Don't think
I'm hardhearted. (*Brother with one sister*)

When she's ill she'll stay in bed. She won't come here.
At times I'll insist, "You're coming here." I had her here
after the gall bladder surgery for six or seven weeks.
(*Sister with two brothers*)

A few years ago Mother had a bad back. My father refused any help, and it was a horrible situation. Now we
would tell him we would get someone in. Without his
eyesight he couldn't do it. (*Sister with two brothers*)

When children did push their parents, they paid a price. The brother, whose mother was described in detail in Chapter 2, felt compelled to do things against her will after she was in an automobile accident in which she was cited for driving without a license. She was under court order not to drive and not to have more than two cats in her home. Previously he had saved her home by paying off some of her debts, in exchange for which he now owned her house. She recently had been diagnosed with Alzheimer's disease. He said:

> She's exceptionally resentful of our assumption of responsibility for her. She's exceptionally resentful of my handling her money. If she remembers and asks about it, the visit disintegrates into a shouting match and I have to leave. (*Brother with one sister and one brother*)

Unlike this mother and other parents with Alzheimer's disease, parents do recover their capacity to resist, something of which their children were mindful.

Pride Mixed with Anxiety

It appears, then, that parents continued to act in what they perceived to be their own best interest, even when it conflicted with their children's views.[97] This was often a source of pride to siblings, but pride sometimes competed with anxiety:

> She had a stroke one and a half years ago, and it has affected her walking. But she gets around, no cane. She refused to use one. She's stubborn. When she's with someone, she does take their arm. One of the things we're afraid of is that she'll fall. (*Brother with two brothers*)

She says, "I'm 91 years old. If I want to take my pills, I'll take them. I'm 91. I'm ready to go. I have no regrets." She just prays she has a peaceful death. That's what she says when we tell her to watch her health. I feel the stress is on me if she isn't well, even though she feels at this age she's lived her life and doesn't need a doctor. (*Sister with four brothers*)

Mother is a very independent and stubborn lady. We've even asked her to let us find a live-in companion. She's embarrassed about the incontinence. She says she has us children and her neighbors, and that's all she needs. And Mother is still the head of the house. (*Sister with one sister and one brother*)

I don't think she'd ever go to a nursing home. She needs somebody to bathe her; she needs somebody to clean for her; she needs somebody to take her places; she needs somebody to do her clothes, but she says she's independent. For years we've been telling her to move. She lives on the second floor. It's a very dangerous situation. She has to crawl up the stairs. She won't listen. You can't tell her. "Who's the daughter? Who's the mother?" is frequently heard around here. (*Sister with two brothers*)

She would never sell her home. She feels she'll never be ill. She's not realistic at all. She won't let us help her. She hasn't even made a will. She won't listen, but she does fine now. She has no sympathy for people who can't do things for themselves. We try to reach her every day. If she doesn't answer, we jump in the car and go to see what's wrong. But, of course, that makes her mad. (*Sister with one sister*)

This last informant's sister said,

She's so independent — that's what worries us. She was burglarized over a year ago. Two men broke in, kept her captive and took her belongings. She said, "I'm going to have a heart attack; you'd better hurry. Would you do this to your mother?" The burglar who was holding the flashlight kissed her when he left. We have tried to get her to live with us since then, but she won't. My sister and I would like her out of the house. She likes her privacy. She doesn't want to be accountable to anyone. She's that independent, and if she doesn't want to answer the phone, she doesn't, which worries us." (*Sister with one sister*)

The siblings, then, and particularly the sisters, given their propensity to monitor, were not always pleased with their parents' decisions; but on the whole they accepted them even when the consequences were extremely inconvenient or worrisome for them.

SOCIAL NETWORKS OF OLD PARENTS

Because most research relies on primary-caregiving children as respondents, rather than on old parents, when social-support networks are examined, it is the adult children's rather than the parents' that receive attention. Again, this is related to the fact that so much of the current research on older families focuses on primary caregivers whose parents are demented. Rarely is the possibility entertained that parents have social-support networks that supplement or are independent of their children.[98] The parents in these 149 older families were assumed to be embedded in networks that included not only their children and grandchildren but others who were tied directly to them. In the open-ended interview, therefore, siblings were asked about ties that their parents might have that were not mediated by them. Specifically, they were asked whether a parent received and/or gave any assistance to their siblings and siblings-in-law, neighbors, friends, church members or members of other organizations, social services, or paid helpers. Siblings were also free during the interview to refer to anyone whom their parents knew and could count on for assistance and companionship. Because these data are secondhand, they probably underestimate the degree to which parents interact with, rely on, and are relied upon by others. Nevertheless, they produce an image of old parents that belies current assumptions that old parents are socially isolated and dependent only on their children to insure that their needs are met.

The discussion of parents' networks focuses on two broad categories of persons that were identified by the siblings. The first includes neighbors, friends, and community; the second, relatives other than adult children.

Neighbors, Friends, and Community

Neighbors were a ubiquitous part of old parents' social networks. Siblings referred to helpful, long-time neighbors.[99] A sister said of her 90-year-old mother, who lived in a single-family-home:

> A neighbor watches and has called me to say, "I haven't seen your mother out." Mother fell when we were in California, and that neighbor did call my daughter. Two neighbors — the lady across the street and the one next door — look out for her and would help in an emergency. (*Sister with one sister*)

A sister whose mother was watched over round-the-clock by two paid helpers, said:

A neighbor comes over two to three times a week to visit. She said that she can see Mother failing, that it's harder for her to carry on a conversation now. Sometimes she brings over food. (*Sister with one sister*)

Even this very infirm parent continued to have an attentive neighbor. A sister said:

Her one neighbor cuts her grass, and another is very nice and looks in on her. I'll call them to ask, "Can you see her?" if I haven't been able to reach her, and they'll tell me she's out in the yard. (*Sister with one sister*)

A sister, whose 92-year-old mother lived in public housing for the elderly and had recently had cataract surgery, said:

Her neighbor's husband does a lot of little things in the apartment when my brother can't come. He will do her eye drops four times a day. We were concerned how it would get done. This is a new thing. She and her husband have been in the apartment two years now. I've never even met him because I'm there at times when he's not. (*Sister with one brother*)

A sister, whose mother had lived with her while recuperating from a stroke but who had returned to live in her single-family home, said:

She cannot possibly live by herself without help. She has wonderful neighbors who help get things out of drawers or if she drops things. Someone does her shopping. Neighbors come in to pare potatoes or chop meat. She has a signal with her drapes in the morning, and the woman across the street knows that if the curtains are open that everything is okay. (*Sister with one sister and one brother*)

A mother living in a "two-family" house lived on the first floor with a tenant above her on the second. Her daughter said:

> She rents her upper suite to a man who would be aware of any problems that might arise. She has spoken to him about the problem. If she bangs on the ceiling, he is to come down. (*Sister with one sister and one brother*)

Siblings also lamented neighbors who had departed, leaving a hole in their parents' networks. A brother said of his mother:

> She's been living alone the last year. Up until last year she had a roomer, but he died. I have more anxiety over that since the boarder died. The only plus in the situation, her doctor lives right across the street, and she's close to his wife and their family. (*Brother with one brother*)

The importance of neighbors was also addressed in Chapter 2, where the significance of parents' residence was discussed.

Some parents were described as long-term members of groups of friends who spent a great deal of time together and watched out for one another:

> My father's failing health was hard for my mother. She and my father and three other couples moved down to Florida together. They helped her with his care, shaved him, etc. Now they are all very supportive of her. (*Sister with one sister*)

> Father and Mother have a large support group here, with whom they've grown old together. They're in an apartment in which the management representa-

tive — he's more than just a custodian — is always on
the premises. When we go to town at Christmas, we
stay at our parents' friends who are gone. They're very
active socially with couples and singles who used to
be couples, a large inner support group. (*Brother with
one brother*)

In addition to specific neighbors or close friends whom
their parents knew, siblings also mentioned neighborhood
and community resources on which their parents relied.
Distant children mentioned the importance of the community in which they had grown up and their parents still
lived:

Mother lives 700 miles from me, 500 from one sister,
and 250 from my other sister. She does live in a village
with extended family and a lifetime of friends. There's
her hairdresser who she goes to every week. April takes
her in the car. Mom pays her. April is a person my age,
but a friend, and Mom gives her a token to cover her
expenses. I think they swing by the grocery store then,
too, and once in a while into the county seat to make
major purchases. I think she has a back-up person in
case April can't drive. She also pays someone to mow
her yard and a high school girl to come in to vacuum
and dust once or twice a month. She has nephews
and nieces who'll come to clean out the basement
and things like that. (*Sister with two sisters*)

A brother described his parents' position in the small town
in which he had grown up:

They live in a small town and know people. They're
involved in church and the lodge. All of her sisters and
brothers live within a twenty-mile radius. There's a lot
of familial support, almost a clannish operation. They
look after each other and each other's kids. Mother fell
about six months ago and broke her foot. She volun-

teers at the County Hospital as a gray lady, so she was treated free at the hospital. Mother also used to work for the police department. She would call them [if she locked herself out of the house]. They're well known in town. (*Brother with two brothers*)

One brother described his mother's community as a "small, very friendly southern community" (*Brother with one brother*).

In urban areas neighborhoods were described as important for parents. A sister, whose mother was receiving a great deal of support from her and her sister, pointed out why it was more advantageous for her mother to live with her sister rather than with her:

The location of my sister's house is important to my mother. It is in her old neighborhood near Mother's church and her pupils. She still teaches some students the piano. She's been a member of the church for forty years, and they had a big party for her at the church. She's very active in the choir and church guild. (*Sister with one sister*)

Another sister said that her mother's neighborhood provided access to activities and services:

The minister is like an adopted son. He gives her rides, and she calls him to talk to him. He'll get after her for walking to church instead of getting a ride. He'll call me sometimes to talk about her. She's the oldest member of our church, and they try to look after her in small ways. She goes to the senior citizens center to eat lunch. It gives her a chance to visit with others her age. There's a foot doctor there and an eye doctor, all through that center. (*Sister with five sisters and one brother*)

One sister referred indirectly to the neighborhood her mother lived in:

> She has a dog and walks her four or five times daily, and she keeps fit this way. She is very attached to the dog emotionally, and it makes her very happy. It took her about four years to get back on her feet emotionally after my father's death, but getting the dog ultimately made the difference. (*Sister with one sister and one brother*)

Availability of public places in which parents apparently felt comfortable also was mentioned as an asset of neighborhoods and communities. Describing her recently widowed father, one sister said:

> There are lots of lonely times in the winter, but he's dealing with it. Ponderosa has a fabulous brunch. He gets a paper and gets breakfast, and it takes him an hour and a half. (*Sister with two sisters*)

Community and neighborhood resources in the form of both individuals and familiar places were mentioned by some siblings as important sources of support for their parents.

Relatives

Siblings also described parents' immediate family members as belonging to their parents' social networks.[100] Parents' sisters were especially prevalent:[101]

> My mother's sister, who is five or ten years younger, lives next door. They built this duplex fifteen to twenty years ago with the idea that they would live next door

to each other. It has worked perfectly for them. She's happy with her living situation. She has privacy and her own domain, but she's right next door to her sister. (*Sister with one sister*)

She has a close support network with her and her two sisters. They're very close and have been all their lives. Their lives pretty much revolve around each other. They call each other almost every day. Two of them are in very good health, including my mother. She's young for her age [77]. Her two sisters are in the Cleveland area. Also, there's a sister-in-law she's very close with, but I don't think she talks with her every day. I can't see her leaving Cleveland for too long. She has that support system — not only her sisters but also friends, a *lot* of friends. She really doesn't like to be away. (*Brother with one brother*)

My mother's half-sister in New York still has contact with her. This sister's daughter and family are in Cleveland. (*Brother with one brother*)

My father's sister lives nearby and was of a lot of help during Mother's recuperation from a broken hip. (*Brother with two brothers*)

My mother's sister checks on her daily by phone. (*Sister with one brother*)

She talks to her sister every day on the phone. She doesn't see her in the winter, but in the summer she sees her once a week. (*Sister with one brother*)

Parents' brothers also contributed:

> My father's brother gave him a "grant" at one time to
> help pay for his care at the retirement home. (*Brother
> with one brother*)

A brother said, "Mother gets some help financially from me
and my two uncles" (*Brother with one sister and one brother*).
His sister also reported this: "Her brothers help pay her rent.
They have been doing it for the past thirty-one years. They
promised my mother they'd do it" (*Sister with two brothers*).
More distant relatives also were described as members of
their parents' social networks:

> My mother goes to senior groups two or three times
> a week, usually with my cousin, my mother's nephew,
> who is retired as well. He lives about two blocks away.
> (*Brother with one brother*)

A sister and brother described their cousins' involvement
with their father:

> Actually, a couple of my father's nephews, now retired,
> are like sons to him. They give him rides. They're very
> close to him. They have been very nice. (*Sister with
> one brother*)

> My father is the last of five children, but the children
> of his siblings are still in Cleveland. They are close to
> him. He probably knows them better than his own
> family. They're like a second family to him. (*Brother
> with one sister*)

Research on older families rarely includes extended kin. The
variety of kin who are potential members of parents' networks makes asking about specific relatives too cumbersome
for fixed-choice questionnaires. This leaves the impression
that old parents rely exclusively on their children. In this

study, open-ended interviews made it possible to draw attention to parents' supportive relationships with relatives
other than their children.

Another category of relatives that was mentioned by some
siblings were partners of parents — new spouses, as well as
girlfriends and boyfriends. Although stepparents were not
always welcome additions to the family, siblings nevertheless
saw their contributions as important to their parents:

> I don't get along with his wife. She's just a bitch, but
> she's wonderful to my father. (*Brother with one sis-
> ter*)

> My father started going with his girlfriend two weeks
> after Mother died. I resented her a great deal, but now
> I'm glad she's there. (*Sister with one sister and two
> brothers*)

> He has a lady friend who brings him meals four or
> more times a week. (*Sister with two sisters*)

> This is Mother's third husband. He's 10 years younger
> than she is and able to do things. (*Sister with one sister
> and two brothers*)

One brother reported that his 80-year-old mother, after having been divorced for more than thirty years, was about to
marry an old friend (*Brother with one brother*).

Looking beyond the care provider to the parent's social
network challenges the current research practice of focusing exclusively on the social-support networks of adult children. Largely because those with Alzheimer's disease have
received the most research attention, parents are presumed
to be isolated when, in fact, many are not. Even when par-

ents were not "easy to have a conversation with," associates whose relationships with an old parent were not mediated through their adult children continued to attend to them. While there is no question that having supportive children is an important resource, old parents have other resources that contribute to their independence and self-sufficiency.

Parents were brought into the division of family labor in this chapter. Too often in research on older families, old parents are relegated to passive roles in which their influence on their children is assumed to be exclusively in terms of their care requirements. The data provided by the siblings in these 149 families, however, made clear that parents had a great deal to say about how family labor was divided and what contributions were acceptable. They were far from passive recipients of their children's ministrations. They orchestrated contributions and actively and passively resisted their children's advice. Siblings described resorting to manipulation and subterfuge to "put one over" on their parents, a clear sign of who was in control. Siblings spoke of "allowing" their parents to do things their way, but this choice of words seemed to belie the actual position of the siblings in the decision-making process. Parents were very much in charge. They also were embedded in social networks that went beyond the siblings. These networks included friends, neighbors, community resources, as well as other relatives whose ties were not mediated by their children. Siblings mentioned these ties both in response to direct questions and spontaneously during the interviews. Again, it is important to remember that because these data are secondhand, they probably underestimate the degree to which parents interacted with, relied on, and were relied upon by others.

Now that all parties have been introduced, the topic of conflict and tension about the division of family labor can be broached. Structural features of families and relative attributes that led to tension are described in the following chapter.

Chapter Seven

Sources and Management
of Family Discord

This chapter focuses on factors that led to discord among siblings as they performed the family labor of meeting their parents' needs. In other research "primary caregiver" respondents often accuse their siblings of not supporting their efforts. They also report that siblings spend less time with their parents and perform fewer tasks.[102] It was somewhat surprising, then, that in these 149 families there were few assertions that the division of labor was unfair; nor was there a great deal of expressed animosity. When siblings used one or more of the eight attributes identified in Chapter 4 to explain their relative contributions to parents, their explanations were *not* routinely accompanied by accusations that a sister or a brother was behaving inappropriately, even when the division of labor objectively was grossly unequal.[103]

Siblings were not universally pleased, however, with one another's participation in the family labor of meeting parents' needs. Most notable with respect to discord were mixed-gender sibling groups, especially those that included a lone sister. In addition, discord stemmed from siblings' not honoring the rules for the division of labor that their relative statuses seemed to dictate. Hence, groups in which some members were essentially equivalent but did not participate equally often included one or more disgruntled sibling. The negative effects of failing to follow rules were also obvious in disagreements between siblings who lived near their parents and those who lived too far away to participate routinely. This chapter concludes by focusing on explanations for the apparent low level of discord in most of these families. By following implicit rules that arose from their collective statuses, siblings were able to manage conflict. Furthermore, some siblings, particularly sisters, were mindful of their relationships with one another and took care to protect them.

Size and Gender Composition
of Sibling Groups

To recapitulate the findings presented in Chapter 5, in single-gender groups, siblings were likely to have similar views about the appropriate way of meeting parents' needs. Pairs and groups of sisters expected to coordinate their actions and accepted parental dependency; pairs and groups of brothers promoted their parents' independence and, except in times of crisis, did not expect to work in concert. In mixed-gender sibling groups, sisters and brothers often did not appreciate one another's approach.

Lone-sister sibling groups were the most vulnerable to discord. As the sole expert on family matters in her generation, a lone sister expected to take the lead and organize efforts to meet parents' needs. To sisters' annoyance, brothers were often reluctant followers. One sister described her

routine involvement with her mother and her brother's unwillingness even to be her back-up:

> If I need something for Mom, he will help if I ask, but
> only if I ask. He may not always agree with my course
> of action, but I make the final decision. He may do this
> or that, like he cut the hedges, but he left the branches
> on the ground. (*Sister with one brother*)

In his interview her brother also referred to this incident: "I
pruned the trees last week, but she said I did it wrong." In his
opinion his sister was *too* involved in their mother's life:

> I think that, given the fact that my mother has live-
> in help, my sister doesn't utilize it as she should. She
> feels no one can do it like she can; consequently all the
> burden falls on her. (*Brother with one sister*)

According to both the sister and the brother, his contributions to his mother were minimal:

> I visit my mother and do some very minor things, er-
> rands, etc. My sister is upset because I don't play an
> active role. Mostly I just visit and take care of minor
> things — business matters, real estate. (*Brother with
> one sister*)

Both he and his sister viewed these "circumscribed" contributions as relatively inconsequential. When he did do
something, he was viewed by his sister as being more of a
nuisance than a help, something she apparently made plain
to him. He explained or complained (which is not clear): "My
sister manages it pretty much herself." The sister expected
her brother to do things her way, to back up her routine
involvement. With the live-in help in place, he expected to
be involved directly with his mother as an obedient son.

To the question, "Do you think too much burden falls on you or any of your brothers?" the only sister in a group of five siblings responded:

> Too much falls to me. I don't think any of them are doing their fair share. Money doesn't take the place of giving of themselves. Compared to what they are doing, which is really nothing but money, I'm doing too much. All of the work is left to me. I don't feel that this is fair, but I have learned to accept it. (*Sister with four brothers*)

Knowing that her brothers' approach was to pay someone to provide services to their parents, her response was to "do too much" herself: "If they ask me if things are being done for our parents — if I were to say, 'No, I'm not doing it' — they would get someone to do it." Unwilling to see her brothers' solution as acceptable, she adapted by doing herself what she believed was necessary.

One of her brother had a quite different view of the fairness of the division of family labor:

> My sister has become Mom's closest friend. Dad will bring her to the house. When Mom is sick she goes by one or two days a week and Sunday. My oldest brother is the administrator of finances and the executor of the will. He knows a lot of business law. He also helps with anything about stocks and bonds. I am more in charge of quick turnover money, like what parents would do with a lump sum that would have a quick turnover. But he does long-range planning about money. Also, I am the one who visits all of our relatives. My youngest brother has the most difficulty with Dad and is the closest to Mom. He helps out with moral support. He helps with jobs as they come up. In an emergency they would call either me or my oldest brother because we are the most flexible in schedule. No one organizes

it. My oldest brother and I have influence with Dad. We see him most often. One brother is in Ashtabula, and my youngest brother doesn't have closeness with Dad. My sister will shop for Mom. That's something she likes to do. We do what we are good at — and convenience, like who is closest, of course, they see them more often. We all do the best we can. We don't ever mind what we do. I think it's fair because it falls along the lines of interest and ability. (*Brother with one sister and three brothers*)

In response to the question, "How would things be different if you had another sister?" he said:

I guess a lot of what my sister does would be split. I don't think she would see less of our parents, especially Mom. She visits because she likes to. Dad would still insist on doing everything. (*Brother of one sister and three brothers*)

Unlike his sister, then, he did not think she was doing more than her fair share. He viewed the contributions of each of his siblings as appropriate and took gender differences as simply given. The sister, but not her brother, was unhappy with the division of labor. Her brother assumed that she would ask for help if she was unhappy. The sister, however, regarded the help likely to be proffered — hired assistants — as unacceptable.

A brother in another family explained that he and his sister did not always see eye-to-eye:

My sister and I have never sat down to talk about it specifically with any concrete planning. We talked about Mom's hearing and Dad's work; however, we came to no conclusions. We have some difficulty talking about these things. She's a great gal, but there is a certain degree of rivalry. She wants it to be her idea.

> She always wanted to protect my parents. She's the
> caretaker of the family. We are always dealing with
> leadership instead of what are we going to do with the
> folks. There is a lot of diplomacy. We haven't gotten
> around to what can be done when and if something
> happens to them. The discussion is never a discussion,
> just a superficial statement. I think she feels she has a
> monopoly on the way to handle my parents and things
> in general. (*Brother with one sister*)

He diplomatically resisted his sister's attempts to make him
see things her way. He and his sister lived in Cleveland, their
parents two hours away, making implementing his sister's
ideas difficult. This, in addition to the fact that their parents
were still fairly self-sufficient, staved off discord.

Sisters in mixed-gender sibling groups that included
two or more sisters were likely to share an approach and
could more easily accommodate the different approach of
their brothers. They typically were less critical of brothers
who resisted attempts to incorporate them routinely in the
division of labor. A 92-year-old mother lived in an apartment complex for seniors near two sisters. One sister said
that their mother was "very active, much against what we
would like." The two sisters were routinely involved in her
life. One sister explained how she and her sister worked
together:

> It's equal for both my sister and me. If something came
> up, my sister would say, "I'll do it," and I'd say, "No, I'll
> do it." And one of us just would. We share responsi-
> bilities, but not on a prescribed basis. (*Sister with one
> sister and one brother*)

Their brother lived in New York State:

As far as my brother is concerned, he's lived out of town for so many years, he's really not in the picture from day to day. He calls Mother all the time but doesn't have regular responsibilities in this situation. (*Sister with one sister and one brother*)

Her sister, however, expressed concern that her brother was not as attentive to their mother as she would have liked:

I did phone him a few months ago to bring him into it, to ask him specifically to come to visit. It helps to calm her down. I'd feel bad if something happened and I hadn't called him. He doesn't make much contact on his own. (*Sister with one sister and one bother*)

The sisters neither expected their brother to be involved routinely nor held it against him that he was not "in the picture from day to day." Instead, they supported one another and "brought him into it" when one of them deemed it important.

Not all pairs of sister, however, were as forgiving of brothers who preferred to go their own way. In a family of two brothers and two sisters, the two sisters shared their mother's care and their unhappiness with their local brother who refused to follow their lead. Their out-of-town brother was held to a different standard. Their infirm but mentally competent 97-year-old mother had exhausted her funds and depended on them to pay her rent in a retirement hotel. The two sisters cooperated; arranging vacations to avoid being away simultaneously; and shared everyday errands, visiting, and appointments. Both described their two brothers as minimally involved:

> Communication, visiting, concern are responsibilities
> that my older brother doesn't meet. He doesn't share
> the concern with us . . . my younger brother who lives
> in Kansas City is a softer kind of person, and if he
> were in Cleveland it would be different. I could ask
> him anything, and he will do it. (*Sister with one sister
> and two brothers*)

According to her sister, since her mother's finances had run
out, "It's been particularly bad with my older brother. My
younger brother does help." Note that the brother who does
not live in town is forgiven for not participating, while the
brother who lives in town is not.

A recent disagreement between the two sisters and their
older brother stemmed from a visit to a nursing home to
which they thought their mother might move:

> The place where my mother would live — the most
> ambulatory — people were in wheelchairs, walkers.
> People were sleeping. It was awful. My mother is not
> like that. She's active. My brother was convinced that
> this was the place for my mother. He had to leave be-
> fore the tour. My sister called him later and said this
> was not the place for Mother. He was upset because
> he disagreed. We told Mother later we had been there
> and this was not the place for her. (*Sister with one sister
> and two brothers*)

The two sisters, then, were angry with their proximate, older
brother who failed to participate as they expected in meeting their mother's needs. They rejected his wish to move
their mother to a setting in which she would have required
fewer services from her children. In all likelihood she also
would have been eligible for Medicaid, thereby relieving

the siblings of financial responsibility as well. Both of these probable consequences are in keeping with brothers' typical approach. The two sisters supported one another's view that their local brother was filially irresponsible. By the same token their willingness to accept their mother's dependence on them prevented their brother from meeting his mother's needs in a way he felt was appropriate.

Because women traditionally have been viewed as experts on family matters, sisters felt they knew how to meet their parents' needs better than their brothers did. They expected their brothers to cooperate with them, if not routinely, at least as backup. Brothers, however, often were unwilling to acknowledge that their sisters' approach, which accepted dependency, was better than theirs, which promoted self-sufficiency. Lone sisters, then, were in the difficult position of trying to induce brothers, their only available siblings, to follow their directives. To do so, brothers would have had to see themselves in relation to their sisters, rather than exclusively in relation to their parents, and to acknowledge that their sisters knew how to meet their parents' needs better than they did. Some brothers were simply unwilling or unable to do so. By the same token brothers whose sisters believed that dependency was acceptable were prevented from encouraging their parents' self-sufficiency. They were precluded from contributing in ways they believed were appropriate, especially as parents needs increased and parents were not discouraged by sisters from becoming more dependent on them. In their turn, sisters viewed their brothers as shirkers.

Avoiding Potential Conflict

between Sisters and Brothers

Discord in mixed-gender sibling groups stemmed from disagreement between brothers and sisters about the best way to meet parents' needs. Even in lone-sister families, however, bitter complaints about siblings' contributions were not common. Four factors mitigated discord even in lone-sister sibling groups. First, some brothers were willing to follow a sister's lead. One lone sister explained how she and her unmarried brother divided responsibility for their widowed mother, who lived alone on two acres of land ninety miles away from the city where both siblings resided. At the time of the interview, the brother was living with his sister, having changed jobs to move to the Cleveland area to help his sister meet their mother's needs. His sister said:

> My brother and I are both available. I'm available more for evening emergencies, but if necessary I would go. He could go during the day now. He is working four days a week. I organize it. I ask him to do things for Mom. He and I both do what we can to help her. He makes every effort to take on half the responsibility. I'm the one who initiates things, and we work together. (*Sister with two brothers*)

Her brother concurred:

> One or the other will do things. We try to lift the load. My sister takes her sick days or days off to help Mother. My sister had done most herself; now I'm in the area trying to relieve her. (*Brother with one sister and one brother*)

This brother willingly followed his sister's plan. He saw his responsibility as familial rather than filial, that is, as assisting his sister as much as helping his mother. He was willing to adopt his sister's approach to meeting their mother's needs. The result was that the sister and brother worked amicably as a team and split the work as evenly as possible. Some brothers, then, were willing to provide back-up and even routine involvement.

Second, the size of the lone-sister sibling group affected the likelihood of discord. Lone sisters with more than one brother were less likely than those with only one brother to express dissatisfaction with the division of labor. They had two advantages over sisters with only one brother. They were more likely to find one brother whom they felt backed them up. The nonproximate brother of the sister-brother pair described immediately above was not involved with them in providing services to their mother. Although both his sister and his brother indicated that he was in communication with their mother, the sister said, "He doesn't want to be involved in someone else's problems." From the sister's perspective, of her two brothers, one at least was supportive of her efforts.

Even if no brother was willing to serve as a "back-up," from a lone sister's perspective a larger number of brothers meant that there simply were more hands, even if those hands did not necessarily follow orders. Especially if the brothers lived nearby, they at least interacted with their parents even if, in their sisters' view, their contributions were "sporadic" or "circumscribed." A sister with five brothers said: "That's one nice thing about a big family. One person is not burdened with doing it all" (*Sister with five brothers*). When asked how things would be different if she had a sister, one lone sister said, "I just feel it would be one more person to help, but I don't necessarily feel that it would ease the responsibility, because there are so many of us now" (*Sister with four brothers*).

Third, not all lone sisters held an "egalitarian ideology." Some did a great deal more than their brothers for their parents without protest, because they were daughters. They were content to be "traditional." By the same token their brothers were likely to respond to their requests much as traditional husbands "help" their wives.[104] The ever-single sister with four brothers, cited immediately above, lived with her 91-year-old widowed mother. She said: "I think I'm doing much more than my brothers, but it's fair. I'm doing it all because I'm living with my mother. They have their lives but are willing to help whenever I need them."

Fourth, in some lone-sister families, attributes other than gender differentiated siblings as well. In one family a brother lived with his mother, while his sister lived 2000 miles away. He did a great deal more for their mother and, although his sister was concerned that her absence affected her mother negatively, she was in no position to call the shots. Her brother was free to be an "obedient son" to his mother. As a nonproximate lone sister, she was not in a position to implement her "superior" knowledge on family matters. She indicated in the interview that if a time came when her mother needed more help, she was prepared to send money.

Siblings in mixed-gender groups, especially lone-sister ones, were the most likely to report discord. Gendered approaches to meeting parents' needs sometimes led to strong disagreements when a sister felt obligated to do a great deal more than her brother(s) in order to insure that things were done "right." But even in lone-sister sibling groups, brothers were sometimes persuaded to follow their sister's plan. Other sisters accepted their traditional role as family caregivers and saw as appropriate asking their brothers to perform "masculine" tasks rather than to share responsibility equally. In addition, difference in geographic proximity to parents highlights the meaning of the phrase "all things being equal." Meeting parents' needs was expressed in a context in which siblings often differed on other characteristics as well, making moot differences in gendered approaches.

VIOLATIONS OF THE NORMATIVE ORDER

Chapter 4 presented evidence that siblings explained their own and their sisters' and brothers' contributions to the family labor of meeting parents' needs by taking into account the relative statuses of sibling-group members primarily on seven attributes in addition to gender. These attributes are proximity to parents, employment status and job characteristics, marital status, responsibility for other family members, health status, social class and discretionary income, and seniority. Respondents accepted as reasonable, for example, that a sibling who lived farther from parents should contribute less than one(s) who lived closer; that an employed sibling should do different if not fewer things than one who was not; and that a sibling who had small children should have different involvement with parents from one whose children were grown. In essence, siblings took into account their relative standings on these attributes to explain not only who did what but why it was reasonable. They were not necessarily pleased with the current division of family labor, but many of them presented it as "making sense under these conditions." In some groups, however, discord arose because the division of labor dictated by their collective statuses was circumvented: the "shoulds" that emerged from the comparison of their attributes were not followed by one or more siblings.

Identical Siblings

The smaller the collective differences between or among siblings on the various attributes, the more equal the division of family labor *should* have been and the more difficult it was to see as legitimate unequal participation. Discord arose when members *with few status differences* participated unequally.

Siblings in some groups in which there were few differences divided family labor equally and had no complaints about one another's participation. One 85-year-old mother had lived in a house between her two sons for more than twenty years. She had been widowed for five years. One brother described his mother:

> She takes care of herself mainly. She's crippled with arthritis and needs a walker to get around. She lives alone in the house next door, and we go over there at least twice a day. I go over there myself every night after dinner for coffee and talk to her just like I did when my father was alive. (*Brother with one brother*)

The two brothers did a great deal with and for their mother. One brother said:

> My brother takes care of all her financial doings; banking is one of them. He will do some shopping, take her visiting and to social affairs. He'll get someone to do the repairs around the house. I do approximately the same thing. I do minor repairs — plumbing — around the house. (*Brother with one brother*)

The other brother reported similar contributions:

> We're both available at all times. We kind of share some things, but basically we're available for whatever

> she needs and our wives also. My brother will do a lot
> of her shopping because he goes every Thursday with
> his wife; and whatever she needs in between, my wife
> or I will get. We try from a conscientious standpoint
> to each take up some, so it's not all put on one family.
> Our mother's interests and needs are really paramount.
> (*Brother with one brother*)

These two brothers (and their wives) shared equally the
family labor of looking after their mother.

With respect to the eight attributes, these two siblings
were almost identical. They lived equidistant from their
mother, in this case very close. Both were employed. Both
were married. They differed with respect to responsibility
for other family members. One had one child, the other
six. All children were adults, but one brother had a de-
velopmentally disabled adult child who required constant
supervision and lived at home. His wife was described as
doing less for the mother than his brother's wife because
of her responsibilities for the dependent adult child: "My
wife will go over two to three times a day. My sister-in-law
will also, but less often. She has so many problems with the
girl." No health problem for either brother was mentioned
nor was any difference in financial standing. When their
father was alive, he had given money to his sons in equal
amounts. The two siblings were brothers, so that they were
affected similarly by gender-role expectations. With respect
to seniority both brothers viewed the older brother as the
leader. The younger one said, "She would call my brother
first about a problem." His brother agreed: "I, being the
oldest, kind of oversee things to a degree."

Although each brother stressed throughout his interview
that they did not consciously divide responsibility for their
mother equally, each did approximately half of the family
labor. Had one brother refused to do his half, the situation

would have been less amicable, unless an attribute could have been identified on which the brothers were dissimilar enough to justify the lax brother's behavior.

In fact, unequal contributions in sibling groups by members who were almost identical were associated with discord. In a family of three sisters, all married and living in the Cleveland area, the two sisters who were interviewed agreed that the third sister was shirking her responsibilities. Their physically and mentally hampered 85-year-old mother lived in a house that the three sisters owned. A nurse had been hired to live with her. One interviewed sister, who worked in sales, lived closest to their mother; the other interviewed sister, less than five minutes from her; and the third sister, three miles away. The last two sisters were not employed. The interviewed sisters both said that labor was divided between the two of them:

> My sister and I share everything. My other sister, nothing. My sister keeps the books, takes care of shopping, Medicare forms. I drive her, take her out to the doctor. At least three times a week, I take her for a ride, bring her to my home for a different atmosphere, to the beauty shop, and shopping for clothes. If problems arose she would call my sister first. She is home and I work. She would be the one to go over there during the day. I am pretty free in the afternoons and I do go over there, too. I'm in sales and my evenings are pretty taken up. My sister is easier to reach in the evenings as well, because I'm out working. My other sister does nothing. She said if she lived closer, she would do more. It's not true. (*Sister with two sisters*)

With respect to their financial situation, one sister said in response to the question of what would happen if their mother's financial need increased: "My oldest sister and I are not able to assist financially. My other sister would have the burden." The sister whom she suggested had more money saw her own financial situation as similar to her sisters': "My two sisters are poor, and I have to help my daughter — who lives with me — and her children." An adult daughter of one of the other sisters lived with her, and the other sister's adult children were out of the house. The sisters rated their own and their sisters' health as "fair." Two of the husbands were described as having health problems.

These sisters, then, on all eight of the attributes were very similar to one another. Unlike the brothers described above, however, there was discord in this family according to the two sisters who were interviewed. They were not forgiving of their other sister's apparent unwillingness to be involved with their mother's care. One sister said:

> My oldest sister always was the favorite of my mother and father, a pain to my younger sister and me, and she doesn't want to see much of my mother. It depresses my mother. Mother asked why she doesn't visit. I tell her it's because she doesn't want to come. I realize that my older sister is a selfish girl. We asked her — if you don't want to see her, call her. She says she has high blood pressure. We play bridge once a week. I still see her then. But she hadn't seen Mother for three weeks when Mother went into the hospital. (*Sister with two sisters*)

The other interviewed sister shared her disapproval of the oldest sister's behavior. In response to the question of whether her mother's situation had affected her relationships with her sisters, she said:

> It hasn't affected my relationship with my one sister. We are very, very close. I was very close to my oldest sister, too, but not now. She's not a part of my mother's

being here. She doesn't do anything. She elaborates on what she has done for my mother in the past — she had her over on Sundays and stayed with her for seven months until we could get a nurse this past year.[105] I'm very upset with her. Instead of fighting with her, I just don't contact her. We talk to each other, play cards together, but do not discuss my mother. (*Sister with two sisters*)

The two interviewed sisters were unwilling to see as legitimate what they defined as their oldest sister's failure to shoulder her share of the responsibility for their mother. The three sisters were too similar in status on the eight attributes to justify one sister's not participating in the division of family labor. Although the two interviewed sisters claimed always to have felt closer to one another than to the oldest sister, they both said that their relationship with her had deteriorated when their mother began to require increased services. The two younger sisters were unwilling to accept as legitimate either excuse offered by their older sister — high blood pressure and her earlier disproportionate contribution.

The siblings in each of the two groups described thus far were almost identical on the eight attributes. Other groups of siblings were more differentiated. In a family that included five siblings and a widowed mother, one sister was very unhappy with the division of family labor. One brother and one sister lived too far away to be of help on a regular basis. One brother lived approximately an hour's drive away. Although the more proximate brother did visit their mother once a week, one sister said: "My brother and his wife would be happy to have Mother spend a few days there, but Mother doesn't like my brother's wife, so she wouldn't go there." Her sister was less pointed: "It's a little different with a daughter-in-law." The two proximate sisters, then, were the siblings to whom fell most of the family labor of meeting their mother's needs. The other three siblings had legitimate excuses for not being involved with her on a daily basis.

Their 85-year-old mother, who had returned to Cleveland from Florida five years earlier when her mobility became limited, lived in an apartment building for senior citizens. According to both sisters she had no friends and depended on her family for companionship and services, although she recently had begun going to lunch one day a week at a senior citizens center, an activity arranged by the oldest sister.

The two proximate sisters lived, respectively, fifteen and twenty minutes away from their mother. One was married, lived with her husband and was not employed. The other worked full-time during the day, was widowed and lived alone. Each had a grown child. Both sisters were healthy. One sister was the oldest of the sibling group, the other the middle sibling. The oldest sister visited her mother daily, took her grocery shopping and to medical appointments, and handled finances. On the one hand, she felt that she should do it because her sister worked full-time; on the other hand, she felt that her sister and her mother should be more appreciative:

> Mother relies on us which, lately, I've been resenting mainly because I'm not the favorite,[106] and I'm the one who gives her the most help and attention. I don't begrudge it, but she doesn't appreciate what I do for her. Since my sister's husband died, she goes every day for a meal, but I have to get the food. My sister and I have never discussed the tasks. I would feel like telling her, "I'll take her today, and you take her out tomorrow." I think I would like to divide responsibilities with her, but I can't discuss that with her. (*Sister with two sisters and two brothers*)

She recounted what for her was an unpleasant discussion of her mother's needs with her sister:

> If my sister doesn't tell my mother she's not coming for dinner, Mother will call me worried sick. Once I called my sister to tell her that she should make a life of her own and not spend all her free time with Mother, or else she'd better call Mother every time she doesn't come. In some ways she's like my mother. Some things you can't discuss with her. She was angry when I said those things to her. (*Sister with two sisters and two brothers*)

Her sister was either more circumspect or did not recognize that her sister was unhappy with her:

> My mother cooks, and I do go over for dinner quite often. She likes to do that. She gets aggravated with her health, and it's mostly on my sister's shoulders. Everyone does his fair share, but my sister does a lot. My other sister says that maybe she has taken on too much. (*Sister with two sisters and two brothers*)

This sibling group is highly differentiated. Neither sister had any difficulty explaining why and accepting that the three nonproximate siblings were only marginally involved with meeting their mother's needs. The nearest of the three nonproximate siblings was a brother who lived an hour away and was married to someone the mother disliked, three attributes that provided legitimate reasons for his not being more involved. The two proximate sisters, however, were almost identical. What distinguished them was that the younger was widowed and employed, the older married and unemployed, characteristics that might easily have offset one another.

Discord in sibling groups, then, resulted when siblings who were virtually identical did not participate equally. What constituted identical was not solely objective. Whether and to what degree gender justified differential participation, for example, was a matter of opinion.

Relative Proximity to Parents

Discord also was evident in sibling groups in which a sibling who "should" have done relatively more or less than another did not comply with expectations. This was clearest in groups comprising siblings who lived near and those who lived far from the parents. Geographic distance from parents is an easy comparison to make and interpret. The degree to which the more or most proximate sibling was recognized by the other(s) as being in charge varied. Similar to the cultural belief that the lead of sisters rather than brothers should be followed in meeting parents' needs, proximate siblings felt that their being "on the spot" privileged them. When nonproximate siblings advised proximate siblings about how to meet parents' needs, proximate siblings sometimes were annoyed.

Nonproximate siblings felt at times that more or different things should be done for their parents. A 96-year-old mother had moved in with one of her four daughters six years before the interview. One sister lived nearby, the other two some distance away. The proximate sister said:

> My sister who mother lives with, because we think alike, are very, very close. The other two, we discuss it but reach a dead end because they are out of touch. They visualize the situation like a storybook — sainted mother around to take care of her children. They are company when they come to town. They don't see her

as she is today, at her worst. On friendly matters we
have a lot of fun. But discussions about Mom hit a
snag. My older sister and I tend to suggest practical
solutions. More glamorous, more fun is the attitude
of the other two. (*Sister with three sisters*)

The two nonproximate sisters were judged by one of the
proximate sisters to be unrealistic. Their input was not
sought nor their suggestions accepted.

In one family the sister lived near her mother, and her
two brothers lived out of town. Both the sister and the interviewed brother said that for her daily physical needs, their
mother would call the sister because she lived closer, but
that she depended on the younger brother for emotional
support. The sister said:

She called my brother and sister-in-law when she had
this problem with her bladder. I think it's because she
could get more sympathy from him. If an emergency
came up, she would call me first. It would be me — I'm
here. (*Sister with two brothers*)

Her brother said:

My sister, obviously, is there for day-to-day things.
She calls my mother several times a week. My brother
handles the family estate and advises Mother regarding financial matters. I would be called most likely for
emotional support, since I'm the youngest and needed
her care long after my sister and brother. My sister and
my mother often call me to complain about one another. I seem to be able to settle their little differences.
(*Brother with one sister and one brother*)

His sister had sought counseling to deal with her feelings
about her mother after her father's death. About her mother
she said:

> She is a very devious, manipulative person. She lies, tries to put me on guilt trips, and is very difficult to get along with. While my dad was alive, he acted as a buffer, but with him gone, I have no desire to be with my mother or have much to do with her. She is controlling, dominating, and has inhibited my actions most of my life. (*Sister with two brothers*)

Her older brother, also nonproximate, was executor of their father's estate, a "gender-appropriate" task. Her younger brother, however, provided emotional support to their mother, something that should have fallen to her — the lone sister and most proximate child. Had this sister been nonproximate and one of her brothers been proximate, she might not have felt so put upon, and discord would have been less apparent.

In another sibling group two sisters lived near their parents and one sister lived in Oregon. Their 84-year-old mother had Alzheimer's disease. During the previous year their father had required hospitalization on two occasions. A nurse had been hired to look after their mother and now was a permanent employee. One of the proximate sisters said about her nonproximate sister:

> My sister in Oregon doesn't believe some of what's happening. She's not here and doesn't see it. We've discussed the situation of a nursing home. Now I'm not as close with her. Before I was closer to her. It's as if she doesn't want to be involved. My anger at her is for not wanting to be involved. (*Sister with two sisters*)

In response to a subsequent question about how her parents' situation had affected her relationships with her sisters, she said:

It's strengthened my relationship with my sister who lives here. We talk frankly about what to do. We totally accept each other as we are. It's changed my other sister's and my relationship because of the lack of her support to me and my sister. She's still the same towards our parents. (*Sister with two sisters*)

She was annoyed by her nonproximate sister's failure to acknowledge that her parents' status had changed. Her proximate sister also viewed her nonproximate sister as unsupportive and said that she knew "maybe sixty percent of what's going on." She refrained from confiding in her or seeking her advice.

In another family one sister lived near her mother, the other three siblings out of town. The out-of-town sister who was interviewed said that she and her husband felt that her mother should stay in her own home, while her in-town sister and brother-in-law wanted her mother to move to an apartment. The out-of-town sister described talking to her mother's physician:

I wanted his input on how he saw her medically. I wanted a good evaluation of her mental status. My brother-in-law called him before I came in. He thought my husband wanted Mother to stay in the house, and he and my sister felt she had to be out. Mother had been sick the first four months of this year. My brother-in-law had done a lot to fix up her house. He and my sister saw Mother deteriorating very quickly and felt we didn't understand that. When we came into her home, it was mental stimulation and we weren't seeing things the same way they were. I knew my brother-in-law had called him. It put the doctor in a tough spot, but I was still able to get some basic information, and the doctor seemed to be saying what my husband said — that she should try it in her own house to see whether she can manage. The house is for sale. No one has bought the house. The house needs so much work it's awful. She really doesn't want to sell the house. She denies the help my sister offers; friends take her shopping, but not on a regular basis. Because I don't live here, it takes away from my right to be strong in the decisions. I can't do for her. (*Sister with two sisters and one brother*)

She felt that her sister prevented her from participating in the division of family labor:

My sister does the financial things. She's the executor of the will. She takes care of the house — repair needs, putting it up for sale, doctor's appointments. She does some grocery shopping. She is either not able or willing to delegate responsibility. This is the third time I'm here for a week, and this time she knew about it in advance, but she hasn't delegated anything to me. . . My other sister left Mother one hundred dollars to get her transportation, a driver. When I was here I interviewed a driver for one day a week, for appointments. Mother didn't want her and my sister didn't insist. So she hasn't had this person. It would have happened if my sister had pushed. . . She doesn't see how she could have used others. She sees herself as a martyr. She's the oldest child, and they often feel the responsibility for care. . . One morning my sister called me and told me that my husband had completely ruined her life. There must have been some miscommunication between him and her. She got upset. She understood that he felt Mother could do whatever she wanted, whereas Mother had told my sister that she could make any decisions she wanted for Mother. My other sister's husband also said he felt that Mother wasn't going to be so eager to move out of the house now that Dad was gone. We never all four of us sat down together. (*Sister with two sisters and one brother*)

Her sister said of her three siblings:

> They don't and haven't done anything for her on a regu-
> lar basis. My brother would if he is asked. My younger
> sister gave her money to hire someone to drive her,
> but she is keeping the money to buy a pair of shoes.
> When she moves to an apartment or needs help, I in-
> tend to ask the three of them, and I think they will all
> contribute. I really take care of all arrangements and
> responsibilities, because they are out of town. It's not
> divided because they don't live here. The burden is
> all mine, except that my sister is coming here to take
> my mother to visit relatives. It would be very nice if
> someone else were here to help share, but they don't
> and they can't. It's not fair, inasmuch as I have to do
> everything because they don't live here. If they did, I
> think they would do more in the way of errands and
> visiting, and I could handle the financial end. That is
> the way it would be divided. I feel that I'm not meet-
> ing all of her needs sufficiently. I need physical help for
> her, and that can't work out because they aren't here.
> (*Sister with two sisters and one brother*)

This proximate sister, the only one of four siblings living
near her mother, felt that her siblings had abandoned her
to the task of caring for their mother and, in so doing, had
relinquished their right to "interfere" in the decisions that
she and her husband made.

In another family the parents were in poor health, although the father's better health made it possible for them
to remain in the small home to which they had moved a
decade earlier following his bypass surgery. The nonproximate brother did not agree with his brother's way of dealing
with their parents:

> We badgered them at Christmas about moving. We
> shouldn't have. My brother just wanted to ceremoni-

ously move them but their emotions didn't move at the
same pace as his logic. . . The problem is that they don't
admit that they need help. They will listen to us tell
them about it. They won't follow through. They could
get someone in to cook twice a week or to clean more
often. There are services around. It's real hard for them
to say they need help. . . My brother is very, very logical,
and I'm much more intuitive and emotional. He'll say
they need to make a move. He'll say we'll get a place over
Thanksgiving, prepaint it, tell them they're moving, and
just do it — in four days. His approach is confrontational,
direct. Me, I say, "Wait. Mother and Daddy have opinions. They don't' want to move. You can't just go and
move them like that." I think if I lived there I'd do a lot
more than he does, because I'm single and I feel guilty
about not living there. (*Brother with one brother*)

When the proximate brother was asked if the situation of
his parents had affected his relationship with his brother,
he said:

It was negative influence at first. My brother, as the one
not there, had lots of bright ideas about what should
be done for my parents. Now we understand things
and work together since I told my brother he should
get more involved instead of just giving ideas for me
to carry through on. I told my brother he should be
more involved, and he has done so to the extent that
he can. (*Brother with one brother*)

The "logical" brother who felt that his proximity privileged
him did not appreciate the "bright ideas" of the nonproximate brother.

In sibling groups in which someone who should have
been involved *less* on the basis of relative attributes was
actually *more* involved, or vice versa, discord resulted.
Difference in distance to parents was the most clear-cut

case. The relative weight of the other attributes was more difficult to calculate.

Again, it is important to recognize that, for the most part, conflict was avoided. Nonproximate siblings typically recognized that telling proximate siblings how to meet their parents' needs was a bad idea. A brother lived near his mother in Cleveland and had a sister who lived in California, whom he visited regularly and considered very close. He said that, although he and his sister discussed his mother's situation, "the final solution to any problem rests with me." A sister, whose sister and mother lived in separate apartments in the same building a three-hours drive from her, explained: "Yesterday I took Mother to pick out plants for her balcony. We spent the afternoon potting them the way my mother wanted them. My sister wants them done her way" (*Sister with one sister*). She disapproved of the way her sister talked to her mother, but she said that she was not openly critical of her sister because she could not offer her mother an alternative living arrangement.

PROJECTED FUTURE OF

SIBLING RELATIONSHIP

Siblings typically have very little practice in dividing family labor before their parents are old. When they reach adulthood, they usually move out of their family of origin literally and figuratively. Their relationships with one another continue, but they have no reason to work together to solve problems. Some respondents supported the assertion made by researchers that when old parents require services, siblings are once again drawn together and learn to appreciate one another more:[107]

> I admire my brother who lives with Mother more for being able to do what he is doing. We are closer because we talk about Mother all the time, and he doesn't have a wife, so it makes discussion with us more often. Our relationship has always been good. (*Brother with three brothers*)

Alternatively, they are disappointed.[108] One sister indicated that increased interaction with her sister had changed her view of her: "I don't like the way my sister talks to my parents. It hasn't added to it; it's harmed it [relationship] significantly" (*Sister with one sister*). There was evidence in these families that past hurts were difficult to overcome, but this had been accepted long before meeting parents' needs became an issue:

> My sister and I have very little in common. Mother's situation has not changed that. We are interested in each other and try to keep in touch. (*Sister with one sister*)

Most said that rivalry and the "taken-for-grantedness" of their childhood relationship had been replaced by an adult relationship.

More important was how siblings saw their future relationships.[109] Rarely were sibling groups able to divide responsibility equally. Relative attributes played a major part in members' contributions. Siblings who cared about their ongoing relationship, however, were careful to protect it by defining the division as equitable when it was not, in fact, divided equally.[110] Because of the difference in the approach of brothers and sisters, the importance of protecting relationships was more obvious in sisters' reports, but there was evidence in brothers' accounts as well that they wanted to avoid letting their parents' needs come between them. One nonproximate brother who was very close to his brother explained:

> Our attitude and our behavior toward our parents are similar with my brother being a little more critical, a little more exasperated — again, I think due to proximity. I mean you're dealing with people that are a handful. It's really easier to do from 600-700 miles away. (*Brother with one brother*)

On the other hand, if the projected future of sibling ties was either tenuous or considered unimportant, relative contributions were more likely to be interpreted as unfair.

Siblings who valued their relationships with one another sometimes went to great lengths to describe their relative contributions as fair. One older sister had almost total responsibility for her widowed mother, who lived with her and required round-the-clock care. Her sister lived one half-hour away. Her contribution was to visit regularly. The sister who contributed disproportionately more explained:

> My sister had problems of her own and had an unhappy marriage. She was divorced fifteen yeas ago, bringing up three children in Texas. I would tell her about problems but not really go into it. She had enough problems. When the children were older (seven years ago), she lived here with us for three years. Then she married a wonderful man and has a good job. . . I've been so happy for her for the past two years that I've tried to protect her because she's so happy. She feels guilty because Mother's here, but we cannot share the burden because it's just not right. (*Sister with one sister*)

Sisters, then, besides being more likely than brothers to take siblings into account, were also more likely to consider how the division of family labor affected their relationships.

Early life experiences affected how siblings felt about one another, but how much they wanted to protect their current relationships was clearly important. If the projected future of the relationship was positive, then it was important to define the division of family labor as equitable, even if the division was objectively unequal.[111]

PARTICIPATION OF PARENTS

In the previous chapter on old parents, the argument was made that parents are an integral part of the division of labor as long as they are mentally capable of participating. One piece of evidence was that they directed the delivery of services. Siblings said that they did what their parents asked them to do, and they indicated that their parents tried to be fair. Old parents, then, were instrumental in reducing the potential for discord in their families. In some cases their contributions were obvious:

> If I weren't so concerned about my parents, I would have thrown my sister out many years ago. We've had arguments, and my parents are the ones who step in to mediate. (*Sister with one sister*)

> My father had cancer and had been forewarned and made all the preparations so that there were no problems. We prepared ourselves and her for his death. We all adapted ourselves to the situation to avoid problems. My father sat down with each of the kids separately and we had almost a year to prepare and eliminate any problems. (*Sister with five brothers*)

In most families, however, the influence of the parents was subtler because it was embedded in traditional family interaction. Parents chose whom to ask for what and took into account such things as whom they had asked most recently. They gauged how a specific request would compete with the other commitments in each child's life. As long as parents are capable of orchestrating the division of family labor, for those with relatively good social skills, discord may be avoided. Parents with Alzheimer's disease and others who require extraordinary care have no such skills. Their disease robs them of the capacity to orchestrate how their needs are met. That bad feelings among siblings are frequently reported in the research literature may be in large part a result of the focus on caregiving to parents who have Alzheimer's disease and, as a consequence, can no longer act as the head of the family.[112]

This chapter identified four potential sources of conflict in sibling groups. Two of them are tied to relative attributes. First, because brothers and sisters often had different ideas about the best way to meet their parents needs, mixed-gender sibling groups were the most likely to experience conflict, especially if they included a lone sister and were small. Second, how family labor *should* be divided was a function of gender and the other seven relative attributes identified in Chapter 4. When siblings violated these "rules," then at least one member of the group was likely to be unhappy. A third source of conflict stemmed from siblings' expectations about their future relationship. Those who wanted to protect their relationship considered the effects of the division of labor on their siblings and were willing to see unequal contributions as fair. This was more the case for sisters than brothers because brothers were more likely to view as independent their relationships with their siblings and their parents. Last, whether the parents were still able to participate in the division of labor made a difference. On the one hand, they could act in ways to diminish conflict.

On the other, they required less assistance from the siblings so that traditional family interaction was not radically altered simply because of the parents' ages. Most striking, however, was not the amount of conflict but how little was reported by siblings in these 149 families. Rather than blaming or competing with one another, most siblings reported that the way family labor was divided was fair "under the circumstances."

CHAPTER EIGHT

LESSONS LEARNED

———————

DRAWING ON DATA provided by pairs of siblings in families that included at least one parent aged 74 or older, the previous chapters described how the family labor of meeting the needs of old parents was accomplished in 149 families — 50 with at least two sisters, 50 with only one sister, and 49 with no sister.

Two chapters (2 and 6) focused on parents, the former to provide evidence of the range of parents' needs and the latter to argue that parents, if they were able, continued to be participants in family life and family labor. It was clear that old parents, despite their age, were not homogeneous. To emphasize this, they were divided into three categories — capable, dependent, and in-between. Each group of parents required different responses from their offspring. In Chapter 6 treating parents as recipients of their offspring's ministrations alone was shown to be a mistake.

Four chapters focused on siblings. Chapter 3 described interaction between siblings and their parents, including the kinds of services provided by siblings. It showed the wide range of interactions and services in which adult children and their parents participated. How siblings' spouses participated was also described. Chapter 4 argued that the division of family labor is better understood by focusing on siblings' attributes as relative, rather than only as individual characteristics. Respondents indicated that the significance of such things as distance from parents and employment status was assigned by comparing siblings to one another. For example, an individual sibling's distance from her or his parents was very significant, but the expectation for how he or she would participate was assigned by taking into account how far the other sibling(s) lived from their parents as well. One of the most important relative attributes that affected who did what with and for parents was gender. In chapter 5 evidence was presented that brothers and sisters have different ideas about the best approach to meeting parents' needs and that sisters' approach often trumps brothers' approach. Chapter 7 showed how family structure — gender composition and size of sibling group — and failure to adhere to the division of labor suggested by relative attributes, accounted for discord between and among siblings. Two other contributors to conflict were the projected future of the sibling relationships, which affected the likelihood of mutual support and the willingness to give siblings who did less the benefit of the doubt, and the capacity of parents to participate in family life. In this concluding chapter implications of the findings are discussed.

The first lesson to take from the study is the degree to which the picture of older family life changes when the net is widened to include old parents who do *not* have Alzheimer's disease or other physical problems that require extensive supervision. A second lesson is that, by focusing on families as networks of relationships, a more complete picture of family life emerges than is the case when individuals or parent-child dyads are the unit of analysis. A third lesson is that including men's voices in research alters the picture of family life in subtle but important ways. Injunctions based in each of these lessons are elaborated below.

LESSON 1:

OLD PARENTS ARE NOT BURDENS

Beginning in the 1980s the gerontological and family research literature moved away from studying intergenerational relationships to focus disproportionately on adult children who are "primary caregivers" to impaired parents. Typically, adult-child caregivers are depicted as "burdened" with old parents who require an extraordinary amount of care and cannot participate rationally in its provision because they have Alzheimer's disease or some other form of dementia.[113] The language of burden carries over to situations in which "caregivers" are providing relatively small amounts of help to their parents.[114] An unintended consequence of this narrow focus is undue pessimism about older family life.

Many of the parents in the families included in this study required assistance in their daily lives, but only some of them required custodial care. Furthermore, what siblings did with and for their parents was not considered by them to be qualitatively different from traditional family interaction. By including families in which old parents are not demented and by not labeling interaction as caregiving, a very different and much more optimistic picture of older family life emerged.[115]

This more positive picture of older family life also stems from the study being qualitative. Because "stress" and "burden" are the principal outcome variables in the research literature, adult children are forced to describe their experience in these terms in response to fix-choice questions. Although, more recently, studies have countered this tendency by also asking primary caregivers about positive aspects of providing care,[116] the way in which adult children can express their feelings is still limited. In this study "outcome variables" were not specified in advance but left to the sibling respondents to identify. In the process of telling the interviewers how they and their siblings divided responsibility to meet their parents' needs, they also indicated how they felt about their parents and their participation in family labor.

Most siblings did not characterize their parents as burdens or their responsibilities as burdensome. Instead, they saw what they did as normal family interaction or an extension of it. Some expressed dissatisfaction, less often with parents than with siblings; but among these 149 families discord was rare. They concurred with John Mogey's assertion, cited in Chapter 1, that "amity" characterizes family ties: "Goods and services, money and love, flow from those who control these resources to those who have need of them."[117] Siblings were neither uniformly negative nor uniformly positive about family obligations but, instead, pragmatic. Meeting old parents' needs was simply one of the requisites of family membership.

LESSON 2:

FOCUS ON FAMILY TIES AND NETWORKS

In this study families were considered to be systems whose members take one another into account to accomplish the family labor of meeting the needs of old parents. The data support the argument that family structure of the network — including size and gender composition — and members' relative attributes affect who does what and whether the division of labor is seen as fair — and by whom. The findings make the case that conceptualizing families as relationships rather than roles will lead to better understanding of life in older families. Sons and daughters can be compared, and adult children can be treated as representatives of their generation; but when adult children are members of sibling groups, research findings are unlikely to provide an understanding of *actual* family life.

The research design for this study is in keeping with the recent trend of asking adult children about old parents, rather than asking old parents directly about their needs and how they are met. One assumption in the construction of the interview guide, however, was that old parents could belong to networks that included more people than immediate family members. Siblings were asked specifically about their parents' possible other relationships — friends, neighbors, siblings, and community involvement. Respondents also were afforded the opportunity to mention them without prompting during the course of the interview. This produced evidence that even some of the least self-sufficient parents were not dependent solely on their children.

That the myopia of focusing exclusively on primary caregivers contributes to the negative image of aging is evident in a recent paper that used data from a representative sample of families to examine the "Well-being of Aging Americans with Very Old Parents." The authors conclude:

> Those who must provide assistance to an aging, or even an ill, parent do not draw upon a larger network of social support to ease the burden. Neither their children, other kin, nor friends, increase support for

those facing these pressures. Surprisingly, this is as true for advice and emotional support as it is for material assistance. Persons 55 and older who undertake the challenges posed by care for a very old, ill parent largely do so alone. Until this challenge is ended by the death of the parent and they complete the transition in intergenerational relations, these persons will provide less assistance to their children.[118]

Left out of this gloomy picture of the presumably isolated adult child (who is unfortunate enough still to have a parent!) is any reference to the parents' networks. Findings from the current study indicate that parents' networks are not reduced to ties with their adult children or those who are mediated through them. In all likelihood interviews with parents would have revealed many more sources of social integration and support than the secondhand data that their children provided. Research designed to explore intergenerational relationships that reduce elderly parents solely to recipients of care create an unrealistic picture of what having old parents means to adult children. The authors cited above go on to write:

> What are the overall consequences of having an elderly, sick parent in need of support, with little social support from others, increased conflict with the spouse, and lower social integration for individual well-being? Consistently negative.[119]

Such a dismal forecast strikes unnecessary fear into the hearts of all older family members, parents and adult children alike. Most of the respondents who participated in this study, however, would not characterize the consequences of having old parents as consistently negative to their own well-being.

LESSON 3: INCLUDE MEN

IN RESEARCH ON FAMILY TIES

An assumption largely unrecognized in the caregiving literature is that there is a "best practice" for meeting parents' needs. Disagreement among family members about whether to institutionalize a frail parent is sometimes noted, but that there is a variety of ways to meet the needs of a parent is largely ignored. The views of primary-caregiving children, typically those of daughters, are often treated as gospel. Social scientists share with other members of society the belief that women know best about family matters and, as a result, fail to question what is actually an untested assumption. The author of a recent review of the parent-care literature, for example, summarizes: "Apparently, when it comes to providing assistance to elderly parents, gender role norms are so strong they prevent sons from substituting for daughters. . . ".[120] The author might have written: "Apparently, gender role norms are so strong they prevent daughters from substituting for sons." The fact that the latter statement seems absurd is testament to the fact that daughters' behavior with respect to old parents is the standard against which sons' behavior is judged.[121]

Findings reported here suggest that brothers and sisters have different ideas about the best way to meet their parents' needs, that is, about what constitutes "best practice." Like all gender dichotomies, this one is too strongly drawn: some brothers adopted an approach similar to sisters' and some sisters' approach was similar to brothers'. Nevertheless, there were two distinct approaches, which differed in three ways. First, brothers responded to parents' requests for assistance, while sisters not only responded to requests but also monitored their parents. Second, brothers saw their relationships with each family member as independent of the others, while sisters saw their own contributions to their parents in relation to their siblings' contributions. Simply put, brothers saw their ties to their parents as "filial," while sisters saw their ties as "familial." Third, brothers wanted their parents to be self-sufficient and helped them accomplish this goal; sisters valued their parents' self-sufficiency but were not averse to their increased dependence on them. Privileging sisters' over brothers' approach, then, gives credence to beliefs that monitoring is better than obedience, familial is preferable to filial assistance, and a parent's increased dependency should not be actively discouraged.

Recognition that "best practice" is open to question makes it possible to design research to investigate which practices are better. It also raises the issue, "best" from whose point of view? This approach, of course, calls for giving voice to old parents, instead of relying on their adult children alone to speak on their behalf.

CONCLUSION

Throughout this book research on primary caregivers has been set up as a foil. In so doing the intention was not to disparage such research. Adult children who provide care to needy parents deserve attention, particularly from those whose goal is to improve both the quality of caregivers' lives and the lives of old people who are no longer able to meet their own needs without extraordinary assistance. My concern is that their plight has eclipsed the fact that many old parents and their children escape what increasingly has come to be seen as destiny.

Another aspect of the book, which is in conflict with much of the current literature, is the inclusion of men. That women — wives, daughters, and daughters-in-law — do much more than their fair share of care is a recurrent theme in the research literature. The findings presented here do not challenge but shed light on that assertion.[122] For the most part, brothers did not do as much for their parents as did sisters; but by identifying elements of gendered approaches, an explanation rather than an accusation emerged. Deborah Tannen argues that understanding that women and men have different goals in conversation will improve communication between them.[123] A similar argument is made here. By understanding that men and women have different ideas about how best to deal with family ties, sisters and brothers may be able to avoid discord.

Any relationship has costs and rewards.[124] Family relationships are different from others because they are involuntary. They cannot be easily dispatched when costs outweigh rewards. In fact, the whole notion of relative costs and rewards has no place in the family lexicon.[125] Because death is the only terminator of family ties, family members are destined to live throughout their lives with a certain amount of anxiety that is only somewhat predicable in its association with specific life stages such as adolescence and old age. Parents worry about their children, and when those children becomes adults, they are destined to worry about their parents and siblings. Such anxiety is the fate of anyone who cares about someone else. This fact, of course, should not be interpreted as a rationale for withholding formal support for family labor through social programs. Instead, this book presents strong evidence that family members can be trusted to use such support wisely and well. The adequacy of social programs that help family members assist one another is one of the hallmarks of a truly civilized nation.[126]

ENDNOTES

[1]An early exception is Ethel Shanas et al., *Old People in Three Industrial Societies* (New York: Atherton Press, 1968) for which all members of the adult child generation are included to examine the relationships between interaction between generations and gender composition and size. More recent examples are Eleanor Palo Stoller, Loran Earl Forster, and Tamara Sutin Duniho, "Systems of Parent Care within Sibling Networks," *Research on Aging* 14(1992), 28-49; Douglas A Wolf, Vicki Freedman, and Beth J. Soldo, "The Division of Family Labor: Care for Elderly Parents," *The Journal of Gerontology* 52B(1997, Special Issue):102-109.

[2]See, for example, Emily Abel, *Who Cares for the Elderly? Public Policy and the Experiences of Adult Daughters* (Philadelphia: Temple University Press, 1991); Elaine Brody, *Women in the Middle: Their Parent-Care Years* (New York: Springer, 1990); Maaike Dautzenbert, *Daughters Caring for Elderly Parents* (Maastricht, The Netherlands: Universitaire Pers Maastricht, 2000); Alexis J. Walker, Sally S. K. Martin, and Laura L. Jones, "The Benefits and Costs of Caregiving and Care Receiving for Daughters and Mothers," *Journal of Gerontology: Social Sciences* 47(1992):S130-S139.

[3]See, for example, David J. Mangen, Vern L. Bengtson, and Pierre H. Landry, Jr., *Measurement of Intergenerational Relations* (Beverly Hills, CA: Sage Publications, 1988).

[4]Norbert Elias, *What is Sociology?* (New York: Columbia University Press, 1978), 122-133.

[5]For an early overview of conceptualizations of parent-child relations including filial responsibility see Vern L. Bengtson and Sandi S. Schrader, "Parent-Child Relations" in *Research Instruments in Social Gerontology*, Vol. 2, eds. David J. Mangen and Warren A. Peterson (Minneapolis: University of Minnesota Press, 1982), 115-128. For more recent examples, see Janet Finch and Jennifer Mason, "Filial Obligations and Kin Support for Elderly People," *Ageing and Society* 10(1990):151-175; Gary R. Lee, Julie K. Netzer, and Raymond T. Coward, "Filial Responsibility Expectations and Patterns of Intergenerational Assistance," *Journal of Marriage and the Family* 56 (1994):559-565.

[6]Harry J. Berman, "The Validity of Role Reversal: A Hermeneutic Perspective," *Journal of Gerontological Social Work* 20(1993):101-111.

[7]Melvin J. Lerner, Darryl G. Somers, David Reid, David Chiriboga, and Mary Tierney, "Adult Children as Caregivers: Egocentric Biases in Judgments of Sibling Contributions," *The Gerontologist* 31(1991):746-755; Deborah J. Merrill, *Caring for Elderly Parents: Juggling Work, Family, and Caregiving in Middle and Working Class Families* (Westport, CT: Auburn House, 1997); William J. Strawbridge and Margaret I. Wallhagen, "Impact of Family Conflict on Adult Child Caregivers. *The Gerontologist* 31 (1991):770-777.

[8]See, for example, Constance T. Cager, "The Role of Valued Outcomes, Justifications, and Comparison Referents in Perceptions of Fairness among Dual-Earner Couples," *Journal of Family Issues* 19(1998):622-648; Scott Coltrane, "Research on Household Labor: Modeling and Measuring the Social Embeddedness of Routine Family Work," *Journal*

of Marriage and the Family 62(2000):1208-1233; Marjorie L. Devault, *Feeding the Family: The Social Organization of "Caring" as Gendered Work* (Chicago: University of Chicago Press, 1991); Arlie Russell Hochschild with Anne Machung, *The Second Shift* (New York: Viking Penguin, 1989); Esther S. Kluwer, Jose A. M. Heesink, and Evert Van De Vliert, "The Marital Dynamics of Conflict over the Division of Labor," *Journal of Marriage and the Family* 59(1997):635-653; E. Dianne Looker, "Images of Work: Women's Work, Men's Work, Housework," *Canadian Journal of Sociology* 27(1999):225-254; Susan M. Shaw, "Gender Differences in the Definition and Perception of Household Labor," *Family Relations* 37(1988):333-337; Beth Anne Shelton and Daphne John, "The Division of Household Labor," *Annual Review of Sociology* 22(1996):299-322.

[9] Ethel Shanas, "Social Myth as Hypothesis: The Case of the Family Relations of Old People," *The Gerontologist* 19(1979):3-9.

[10] Eugene Litwak, "Extended Kin Relations in an Industrial Democratic Society," in *Social Structure and the Family*, eds. Ethel Shanas and Gordon F. Streib (Englewood Cliffs, NJ: Prentice-Hall, 1965), 290-323.

[11] John R. Logan and Glenna Spitze, *Family Ties: Enduring Relations between Parents and their Grown Children* (Philadelphia: Temple University Press, 1996).

[12] Sarah H. Matthews and Jetse Sprey, "The Perils of Drawing Policy Implications from Research: The Case of Elder Mistreatment," in *Elder Abuse: Practice and Policy*, eds. Rachel Filinson and Stanley R. Ingman (New York: Human Sciences Press, 1989), 51-61.

[13]John Mogey, "Families: Intergenerational and Generational Connections — Conceptual Approaches to Kinship and Culture," in *Families: Intergenerational and Generational Connections*, eds. Susan K. Pfeifer and Marvin B. Sussman (New York: Haworth, 1991), 52. See also, Tonya M. Parrott and Vern L. Bengtson, "The Effects of Earlier Intergenerational Affection, Normative Expectations, and Conflict on Contemporary Exchanges of Help and Support," *Research on Aging* 21(1999):73-105. Mogey draws on the work of Bernard Farber, *Family and Kinship in Modern Society* (Glenview, IL: Scott, Foresman, 1973), 4, who contrasts amity with functionalism: "The functional approach starts with the supposition that certain activities, necessary for the society to continue to exist, are performed most efficiently by the nuclear family; hence, the nuclear family is ubiquitous as a recognizable, functioning entity. The alternative position starts with the assumptions that people exist as networks of relatives who have claims on one another; it then asks how people use these relatives. The functionalists thus begin with necessary actions, while the alternative is to begin with people who have biological ties" (p. 4). Using this distinction the argument could be made that much of the research on older families uses a functional approach, while this study uses the alternative approach.

[14]Matilda White Riley, "The Family in an Aging Society: A Matrix of Latent Relationships," *Journal of Family Issues* 4(1983):439-454.

[15]Ingrid Arnet Connidis, "Life Transitions and the Adult Sibling Tie: A Qualitative Study," *Journal of Marriage and the Family* 54(1992):972-982; Connidis and Lorie D.

Campbell, "Closeness, Confiding, and Contact among Siblings in Middle and Late Adulthood," *Journal of Family Issues* 16(1995):722-745; Sarah H. Matthews, Paula J. Delaney, and Margaret E. Adamek, "Male Kinship Ties: Bonds between Adult Brothers," *American Behavioral Scientist* 33(1989):58-69; Lynn K. White, "Sibling Relationships over the Life Course: A Panel Analysis," *Journal of Marriage and Family* 63(2001):555-568; Lynn K. White and Agnes Riedmann, "Ties among Adult Siblings," *Social Forces* 7(1992):85-102.

[16]Connidis and Lorraine Davies, "Confidants and Companions in Later Life: The Place of Family and Friends," *Journal of Gerontology: Social Sciences* 45(1992):S141-149; Connidis and Davies "Confidants and Companions: Choices in Later Life," *Journal of Gerontology: Social Sciences* 47(1994):S115-122; Connidis and Julie Ann McMullin, "Social Support in Older Age: Assessing the Impact of Marital and Parent Status," *Canadian Journal on Aging* 13(1994):510-527.

[17]Ellen M. Gee and Gloria M. Gutman, *The Overselling of Population Aging: Apocalyptic Demography, Intergenerational Challenges, and Social Policy* (Don Mills, Ontario, Canada: Oxford University Press, 2000).

[18]Hochshild, *The Second Shift*, 1989.

[19]Ruth Schwartz Cowan, *More Work for Mother* (New York: Basic Books, 1983).

[20]Bernice L. Neugarten, "Age Groups in American Society and the Rise of the Young-Old," *Annals of the American Academy of Political and Social Sciences* 415(1974):187-198.

[21] Logan and Spitze, *Family Ties.*

[22] Parents' level of need is typically assessed using a series of statements that are called "activities of daily living" (ADLs) and "instrumental activities of daily living" (IADLs). This method of assessment was originally developed by health-care professionals in the 1960s (Sidney Katz, Amasa B. Ford, Roland W. Moskowitz, Beverly A. Jackson, and Marjorie W. Jaffe, "Studies of Illness in the Aged," *Journal of the American Medical Association*, 185[1963]:914-919). These "activities" have been widely adopted by social scientists as a measure of functional health status. In some research old people are asked to say whether they are able to do each of the tasks independently, only with assistance, or not at all. In other research someone else, usually the primary caregiver, is asked to make the assessment. Responses to the questions typically are summed so that the old person receives a score. In some studies parents who need help with only one activity are considered dependent and those who help them defined as "caregivers." See, for example, Robyn Stone, Gail L. Cafferata, and Judith Sangl, "Caregivers of the Frail Elderly: A National Profile," *The Gerontologist* 27(1987):616-626.

[23] Jessie Bernard, *The Future of Marriage* (New York: World Publishing, 1972).

[24] Carolyn J. Rosenthal, Anne Martin-Matthews, and Sarah H. Matthews, "Caught in the Middle? Occupancy in Multiple Roles and Help to Parents in a National Probability Sample of Canadian Adults," *Journal of Gerontology* 51B(1996):S274-S283.

[25] Michael Young and Peter Willmott, *Family and Class in a London Suburb* (London: Routledge and Kegan Paul, 1960).

[26] Ethel Shanas, *The Health of Older People: A Social Survey* (Cambridge, MA: Harvard University Press, 1962).

[27] Robert S. Weiss, *Learning from Strangers: The Art and Method of Qualitative Interview Studies* (New York: Free Press, 1994), 23-24, makes a case for "conceptual sampling": "Rather than choose respondents randomly, and thus risk unwanted duplication in our sample, we may prefer to select respondents purposively so that we obtain instances of all the important dissimilar forms present in the larger population. We may further want each of the dissimilar forms represented about the same number of times, so that we have the same knowledge base for each. This kind of sample might be referred to as a sample chosen to maximize range. . . sampling for range will ensure that our sample includes instances displaying significant variation. If we find differences among types of instance, then those differences should hold in a larger population. We will not be able to say anything about the proportion of instances of different types in a larger population since the proportion in our sample might be very different from the proportion elsewhere. But we can say what the various types are like, no matter where they appear."

[28] Amy Horowitz, "Methodological Issues in the Study of Gender within Family Caregiving Relationships," in *Gender, Families, and Elder Care*, eds. Jeffery W. Dwyer and Raymond T. Coward (Newbury Park, CA: Sage Publications, 1992), 132-150.

[29]See Sarah H. Matthews, Margaret E. Adamek, and Ruth E. Dunkle, "Research on Older Families When More Than One Member Responds," *Journal of Aging Studies* 7 (1993): 215-228, for findings based on the overlap between the two projects.

[30]John Lofland and Lyn H. Lofland, *Analyzing Social Settings* (Belmont, CA: Wadsworth, 1995); John V. Seidel, Rolf Kjolseth, and Elaine Seymour, *The Ethnograph* (Littleton, CO: Qualis Research Associates, 1988); Weiss, *Learning from Strangers.*

[31]Lofland and Lofland, *Analyzing Social Settings*, 17.

[32]Logan and Spitze, *Family Ties.*

[33]Candace L. Macken, "Profile of Functionally Impaired Elderly Persons Living in the Community," *Health Care Financing Review* 7(1986):33-49, reported results of the 1982 National Long Term Care Survey which provided a profile of Medicare recipients (95% of the population aged 65 and over) living in the community. The percentage of the population over the age of 64 who reported "moderate" or "severe" impairment in cognitive functioning was 6.3%.

[34]Anne Martin-Matthews and Lori D. Campbell, "Gender Roles, Employment and Informal Care," in *Connecting Gender and Ageing: A Sociological Approach*, eds. Sara Arber and Jay Ginn (Philadelphia: Open University Press, 1995), 129-143.

[35]Bernice L. Neugarten and Dale A. Neugarten, "Aging in the Aging Society," *Daedalus* 115(1986):34.

[36]Macken, "Profile of Functionally Impaired Elderly Persons," 33-49.

[37]Parents were sorted into the three groups — capable, dependent, and in-between — by careful reading of the siblings' descriptions of their parents. The numbers are only suggestive, not definitive, but are included to provide an indication of the distribution.

[38]Unless otherwise noted, data excerpts are from the interviews. Details that might reveal the identity of a respondent have been changed in such a way that the significant information is maintained (e.g., one state substituted for another and one occupation of equal status substituted for another). Notes were taken during the interviews as near to verbatim as possible. The result was sometimes choppy sentences. To make the excerpts more readable, in some cases conjunctions have been added and minor changes made in sentence structure. Occasionally, sentences from different parts of the interview are placed together, in which case ellipses are used to indicate missing words.

[39]For a recent fictional account of this dilemma see Jonathan Franzen, *The Corrections* (New York: Farrar, Straus and Giroux, 2001).

[40]Anne Martin-Matthews, "Intergenerational Caregiving: How Apocalyptic and Dominant Demographies Frame the Questions and Shape the Answers," in Gee and Gutman, *The Overselling of Population Aging,*" 66, writes of the influential books in the field of family gerontology in the mid 1970s: "All of these volumes discussed important issues of the structure of the family, the household and family relations of old people, and health and in-

capacity in later life, and dealt conceptually with many of the same elements of intergenerational exchange and assistance that we continue to examine today. The word 'caregiving' simply did not appear in that literature as a descriptor of the intergenerational relationship. Nor were the roles of 'caregiver' and 'care recipient' described as notable features of intergenerational family relationships either with or between households. The question remains, why the rise of 'caregiving,' and with what consequences?" Katherine R. Allen, Rosemary Blieszner, and Karen A. Roberto, "Families in the Middle and Later Years: A Review and Critique of Research in the 1990s," *Journal of Marriage and the Family* 62(2000):911-926, classified 32.6 per cent of the 908 family gerontology articles they reviewed as "caregiving." See also Sara Arber and Jay Ginn, "The Meaning of Informal Care: Gender and the Contribution of Elderly People," *Ageing and Society* 10(1990):429-454; Logan and Spitze, *Family Ties*; Victor Marshall, Sarah H. Matthews, and Carolyn Rosenthal, "Elusiveness of Family Life: A Challenge for the Sociology of Aging," *Annual Review of Gerontology and Geriatrics* 13(1993):39-72; Glenna Spitze and John Logan, "Helping as a Component of Parent-Adult Child Relations," *Research on Aging* 14(1992):291-312; Alexis J. Walker and Clara C. Pratt, "Daughters' Help to Mothers: Intergenerational Aid Versus Caregiving," *Journal of Marriage and the Family* 53(1991):3-12; Alexis J. Walker, Clara C. Pratt, and Linda Eddy, "Informal Caregiving to Aging Family Members: A Critical Review," *Family Relations* 44(1995):402-411.

[41]"Running through the research literature on families, intergenerational relations, and caregiving is the theme that women are more involved than men in family labor. Women are "kinkeepers" (Carolyn Rosenthal, "Kinkeeping in the

Familial Division of Labor," *Journal of Marriage and the Family,* 47[1985]:956-974). Micaela di Leonardo, "The Female World of Cards and Holidays: Women, Families, and the Work of Kinship," in *Rethinking the Family: Some Feminist Questions,* eds. Barrie Thorne and Marilyn Yolom (Boston: Northeastern University Press, 1992), 252, writes: "We think of kin-work tasks such as the preparation of ritual feasts, responsibility for holiday card lists, and gift buying as extensions of women's domestic responsibilities for cooking, consumption, and nurturance. American men in general do not take on these tasks any more than they do housework and child care — and probably less, as these tasks have not yet been the subject of intense public debate." See also Marjorie Devault, *Feeding the Family* (Chicago: University of Chicago Press, 1991). For social historical accounts of how women came to be the experts on family, see Ruth Schwartz Cowan, *More Work for Mother*; Betty Farrell, *Family: The Making of an Idea, an Institution, and a Controversy in American Culture.* (Boulder, CO: Westview, 1999).

[42]That geographic proximity is an important variable with respect to many aspects of family life has long been recognized in gerontological research. See, for example, Eugene Litwak, "Extended Kin Relations in an Industrial Democratic Society," 290-323. For a more recent evidence, see Bonnie C. Hallman and Alun E. Joseph, "Getting There: Mapping the Gendered Geography of Caregiving to Elderly Relatives," *Canadian Journal on Aging* 18(1999): 397-414; Alun E. Joseph and Bonnie C. Hallman, "Caught in the Triangle: The Influence of Home, Work, and Elderly Location on Work-Family Balance," *Canadian Journal on Aging* 15(1996):393-412; Merril Silverstein, "Stability and Change in Temporal Distance between the Elderly and their Children," *Demography* 32(1995):29-45. For evi-

dence that changing residence is an option exercised as parents' health declines, see Rick S. Zimmerman, David J. Jackson, Charles F. Longino, Jr., and Julia E. Bradsher, "Interpersonal and Economic Resources as Mediators of the Effects of Health Decline on the Geographic Mobility of the Elderly," *Journal of Aging and Health* 5(1993):37-57. See also Jacob Climo, *Distant Parents* (New Brunswick, NJ: Rutgers University Press, 1992) for a creative study of the meaning to adult children of geographic distance from parents.

[43]A consistent research finding is that adult children who live close to their parents talk to them on the telephone more often than those who live far away. This seems ironic if telephone calls are substitutes for face-to-face contact. Apparently they are not. Alice A. Rossi and Peter H. Rossi, *Of Human Bonding* (New York: Aldine de Gruyter, 1990), 372, suggest that the expense of long-distance calls accounts for the difference. Others have suggested that when people live near one another, they may spend time on the phone arranging to meet. In addition, daughters are routinely found to interact with parents on the telephone more often than sons do (Logan and Spitze, *Family Ties*), a finding that is addressed in Chap. 6.

[44]In 1992 in the United States approximately nine percent of men and sixteen percent of women aged sixty-five and older had incomes below the poverty line. Comparable figures in 1959 are thirty-three percent for men and thirty-eight percent for women. Fred Pampel, *Aging, Social Inequality, and Public Policy* (Thousand Oaks: Pine Forge Press, 1998), 4. These figures do not take into account the "near poor" or the distribution of poverty among the aged. As a category, very old women are the poorest.

[45]Peter Townsend, "The Structured Dependency of the Elderly," *Ageing and Society* 1(1981):5-28, points out that social policies are implemented by those who approach clients as members of a category, while family members see old relatives as unique individuals.

[46]Ann Goetting. "Patterns of Support among In-laws in the United States," *Journal of Family Issues* 11(1990), 67-90.

[47]In a review of the literature, Janet Finch, *Family Obligations and Social Change* (Cambridge, MA: Polity Press, 1989), 40, writes, "There is evidence that men, even where they acknowledge that they have responsibilities to parents or children, often exercise those responsibilities through their wives. Sons commonly provide personal care and practical support for their elderly parents through the use of their wives' labour rather than their own." Similarly, Rhonda J. V. Montgomery, "Gender Differences in Patterns of Child-Parent Caregiving Relationships," in *Gender, Families, and Elder Care,* eds. Jeffrey Dwyer and Raymond T. Coward (Newbury Park, CA: Sage Publications, 1992), 70, writes, "Certainly, the integral role of daughters-in-law in parent care is widely acknowledged, and is not matched by an equal involvement of sons-in-law." Deborah Merrill, "Daughters-in-law as Caregivers to the Elderly," *Research on Aging* 15(1993):70-91, describes sons who pass on their caregiving responsibilities for mothers with Alzheimer's disease to their wives.

[48]For an excellent research report on the variety of ways families reorganize following divorce of the middle generation see Colleen Leahy Johnson, *Ex Familia: Grandparents, Parents, and Children Adjust to Divorce* (New Brunswick, NJ: Rutgers University Press, 1988).

[49]Berit Ingersoll-Dayton, Marjorie E. Starrels, and David Dowler, "Caregiving for Parents and Parents-in-law: Is Gender Important?" *The Gerontologist* 36(1996), 483-491; Vira R. Kivett, "Mother-in-law and Daughter-in-law Relations,"18-32, in *Aging Parents and Adult Children*, ed. Jay Mancini (Lexington, MA: Lexington Books, 1989); Nora D. Peters-Davis, Miriam S. Moss, and Rachel A. Pruchno, "Children-in-law in Caregiving Families," *The Gerontologist* 39(1999), 66-75.

[50]For the importance of how siblings' spouses feel about one another, see Graham Allen, *A Sociology of Friendship and Kinship* (Sydney, Australia: Allen and Unwin), 1979. See also Sarah H. Matthews, "Men's Ties to Siblings in Old Age: Contributing Factors to Availability and Quality" in *Older Men's Lives*, ed. Edward H. Thompson, Jr. (Thousand Oaks, CA: Sage Publications, 1994), 178-196.

[51]That family members use various rationales to justify members' participation has been investigated most thoroughly by Janet Finch and Jennifer Mason in a number of publications including, Janet Finch and Jennifer Mason ,"Obligations of Kinship in Contemporary Britain: Is There Normative Agreement? *British Journal of Sociology* 42(1991):345-367 and Janet Finch and Jennifer Mason *Negotiating Family Responsibilities* (New York: Tavistock/Routledge, 1993). Their research focused both on normative and familial justifications. Carolyn Keith, "Family Caregiving Systems: Models, Resources, and Values," *Journal of Marriage and the Family*, 57(1995):179-189, also identifies these justifications as ones used by family members.

[52]Lisa Greenwell and Vern L. Bengtson, "Geographic Distance and Contact between Middle-Aged Children and their

Parents: The Effects of Social Class over 20 Years," *Journal of Gerontology: Social Sciences* 52B(1997):S13-S26.

[53]Eugene Litwak, *Helping the Elderly: The Complementary Roles of Informal Networks and Formal Systems* (New York: Guilford, 1985).

[54]Suzanne Kessler and Wendy McKenna, *Gender: An Ethnomethodological Approach* (New York: Wiley-Interscience, 1978), 18.

[55]Lori D. Campbell and Anne Martin-Matthews, "Caring Sons: Exploring Men's Involvement in Filial Care," *Canadian Journal on Aging* 19(2000):57-79.

[56]Lori D. Campbell and Anne Martin-Matthews "Primary and Proximate: The Importance of Coresidence and Being Primary Provider of Care for Men's Filial Care Involvement," *Journal of Family Issues* 21(2000):1006-1030.

[57]Concern about the effects of women's increased participation in the labor force accounts for a considerable body of research in gerontology. See, for example, Christine L. Himes, "Parental Caregiving by Adult Women: A Demographic Perspective," *Research on Aging* 16(1994): 191-211; Anne Martin-Matthews and Carolyn J. Rosenthal, "Balancing Work and the Family in an Aging Society," *Annual Review of Gerontology and Geriatrics* 13 (1993): 96-117; Eliza K. Pavalko and Julie E. Artis, "Women's Caregiving and Paid Work: Causal Relationships in Late Midlife," *Journal of Gerontology* 52B(1997), S170-S179. Glenna Spitze and John Logan, "Employment and Filial Relations: Is There a Conflict?" *Sociological Forum* 6(1991):681-697.

[58] Sarah H. Matthews, Janet E. Werkner, and Paula J. Delaney, "Relative Contributions of Help by Employed and Nonemployed Sisters to their Elderly Parents." *Journal of Gerontology* 44(1989):S36-S44.

[59] Sara Arber and Jay Ginn, "Gender Differences in the Relationship between Paid Employment and Informal Care," *Work, Employment and Society* 9(1995):445-471. But see Connidis, Rosenthal, and McMullin, "The Impact of Family Composition on Providing Help to Older Parents," 402-419; Martin-Matthews and Campbell, "Gender Roles, Employment and Informal Care," 129-143; Margaret B. Neal, Berit Ingersoll-Dayton, and Marjorie E. Starrels, "Gender and Relationship Differences in Caregiving Patterns and Consequences among Employed Caregivers," *The Gerontologist* 37(1997), 804-816; Andrew E. Scharlach, "Caregiving and Employment: Competing or Complementary Roles?" *The Gerontologist* 34(1994), 378-385. Morton Kleban, Elaine M. Brody, Claire B. Schoonover, and Christine Hoffman, "Family Help to the Elderly: Perceptions of Sons-in-law regarding Parent Care," *Journal of Marriage and the Family* 51(1989), 303-312, asked husbands of caregiving daughters whether their employment was affected.

[60] Francesca Cancian and Stacey J. Oliker, *Caring and Gender* (Thousand Oaks, CA: Pine Forge Press, 2000).

[61] For an overview of gender and labor force participation, see Barbara Reskin and Irene Padavic, *Women and Men at Work* (Thousand Oaks, CA: Pine Forge Press, 1994).

[62] After working with data collected from a very large sample of employed persons who provided information

about their parent care responsibilities, Martin-Matthews, "Intergenerational Caregiving," 75-76, concluded: "The research in which I have been involved for several years strongly indicates that many employees, even those providing quite significant levels of care, for some, the equivalent of an extra day of 'work' per week, do not ask for much in the way of workplace-based assistance. What most desire and welcome is often little more than the understanding and support of a manager or supervisor who has been trained to understand the issues of work-family balance in the context of aging. For others, some options for leaves of absence or flex-time or job-sharing are more appropriate. But the scare tactics of apocalyptic demography have the possible danger of stifling much-needed initiatives in this area."

[63]Eleanor Palo Stoller and Karen L. Pugliesi, "Other Roles of Caregivers: Competing Responsibilities or Supportive Resources," *Journal of Gerontology* 44(1989), S231-S238, make a similar point.

[64]Judith Globerman, "Motivations to Care: Daughters- and Sons-in-law Caring for Relatives with Alzheimer's Disease," *Family Relations* 45(1996):37-45. Nancy Guberman, "Daughters-in-law as Caregivers: How and Why Do They Come to Care?" *Journal of Women and Aging* 11(1999):85-102; Amy Horowitz, "Sons and Daughters as Caregivers to Older Parents: Differences in Role Performance and Consequences," *The Gerontologist,* 25(1985):612-617.

[65]Elaine Brody, *Women in the Middle*; Suzanne Kingsmill and Benjamin Schlesinger, *The Family Squeeze: Surviving the Sandwich Generation* (Toronto: University of Toronto Press, 1998).

⁶⁶See, for instance, Katherine H. Briar and Caren Kaplan, *The Family Caregiving Crisis* (Silver Spring, MD: National Association of Social Workers, 1990). Arguments that the prevalence of burdened caregivers has been exaggerated have been made by Barbara M. Barer and Colleen Leahy Johnson, "A Critique of the Caregiving Literature," *The Gerontologist* 30(1990):726-733; Sarah H. Matthews, "The Burdens of Parentcare," *Journal of Aging Studies* 2(1988): 158-165; Alexis J. Walker and Clara C. Pratt, *Sampling Bias in Family Caregiving Studies: A Research Note* (Paper presented at the Annual Meetings of the Gerontological Society of America, November, 1989).

⁶⁷Laura Spencer Loomis and Alan Booth, "Multigenerational Caregiving and Well-being: The Myth of the Beleaguered Sandwich Generation," *Journal of Family Issues* 16(1995):131-148; Rosenthal, Martin-Matthews, and Matthews, "Caught in the Middle?" S274-S283; Donald E. Stull, Karen Bowman, and Virginia Smerglia, "Women in the Middle: A Myth in the Making?" *Family Relations* 43(1994):319-324; Glenna Spitze and John Logan, "More Evidence on Women (and Men) in the Middle," *Research on Aging* 14(1990):291-312.

⁶⁸Most research on intergenerational mobility focuses on individuals rather than siblings but see Robert M. Hauser, Jennifer T. Sheridan, and John Robert Warren, "Socioeconomic Achievements of Siblings in the Life Course: New Findings From the Wisconsin Longitudinal Study," *Research on Aging* 21(1999):338-378.

⁶⁹In Asian cultures seniority and gender determine who will be primarily responsible for old parents — the first-born son. See Charlotte Ikels, "The Process of Caretaker Selection," *Research on Aging* 5(1983.):491-509. In the United

States the selection process is not as clear-cut. Investigations of the association between seniority or birth order with primary responsibility for old parents has not proved fruitful; but see Julie Robison, Phylllis Moen, and Donna Dempster-McClain, "Women's Caregiving: Changing Profiles and Pathways," *Journal of Gerontology: Social Sciences* 50B(1995): S362-S373; Betsy Bosak Houser, Sherry L. Berkman, and Phil Bardsley, "Sex and Birth Order Differences in Filial Behavior," *Sex Roles* 13(1985):641-651. The data reported here suggest that all things being equal, seniority might make some difference. While siblings continued to think of relative birth order as important, seniority competes with many other attributes that are equally or more significant, geographic proximity, for example.

[70]Michael D. Kahn and Stephen Bank, "In Pursuit of Sisterhood: Adult Siblings as a Resource for Combined Individual and Family Therapy," *Family Process* 20(1981), 86, write: "The new language between siblings, reflecting greater maturity and vastly more sophisticated than that exchanged in their childhood, can be shared and developed for adult dialogue. . . At now similar cognitive levels of development, their new sophistication can help brothers and sisters obtain meaningful information so as to understand and undo past hurts, strengthen old bonds, and develop new ones. The distorted images, or 'frozen misunderstandings,' of their easier relationships can now be challenged and corrected."

[71]Merril Silverstein, Xuan Chen, and Kenneth Heller, "Too Much Of A Good Thing? Intergenerational Social Support and The Psychological Well-being of Older Parents," *Journal of Marriage and the Family* 58(1996):970-982, raise the issue of what constitutes optimal support to old parents.

[72]See, for example, Martin-Matthews and Campbell, "Gender Roles, Employment and Informal Care," 129-143; Eleanor Palo Stoller, "Teaching about Gender," 679-697; Neal, Ingersoll-Dayton, and Starrels, "Gender and Relationship Differences in Caregiving Patterns," 804-816. Some have argued that this difference may stem from the specific tasks about which questions are asked. See, for example, Horowitz, "Methodological Issues in the Study of Gender" 132-150; Carolyn J. Rosenthal and Anne Martin-Matthews, "Families as Care-Providers Versus Care-Managers? Gender and Type of Care in a Sample of Employed Canadians," SEDAP Research Paper No. 4 (Hamilton, Ontario, Canada: McMaster University, 1999). No one has argued, however, that daughters' greater involvement is solely an artifact of measurement. Gary Lee, Jeffrey Dwyer and Raymond T. Coward, "Gender Differences in Parent Care: Demographic Factors and Same-Gender Preferences," *Journal of Gerontology: Social Sciences* 48(1993):S9-S16, suggest another explanation: Mothers are widowed more often than fathers and, therefore, are more likely to require from their children the type of personal care that husbands receive from wives. As a result, daughters *should* be over represented because of the embarrassment that would ensue from a son's providing hands-on care to his mother. However, these researchers found only limited support for the hypothesis that fathers prefer sons and that mothers' prefer daughters to provide their care. See also Sara Arber and Jay Ginn, "Gender Differences in Informal Care," *Health and Social Care in the Community* 3(1995):19-31; Ingrid Arnet Connidis, Carolyn J. Rosenthal, and Julie McMullin, "The Impact of Family Composition on Providing Help to Older Parents: A Study of Employed Adults," *Research on Aging* 18(1996):402-419; Rhonda J. V. Montgomery and Y. Kamo, "Parent Care by Sons and Daughters," in *Aging Parents and*

Adult Children, ed. Jay Mancini (Lexington, MA: Lexington Books, 1989), 213-230; Clare Ungerson, "Women and Caring: Skills, Tasks and Taboos," in *The Public and the Private*, eds. Eva Gamarnikow, David H. J. Morgan, June Purvis, and Daphne Taylorson (London: Heinemann, 1983), 62-77. For the most part, then, the finding that daughters provide a great deal more care than sons do continues to be a "fact in search of a theory," according to Gary Lee, "Gender Differences in Family Caregiving: A Fact in Search of a Theory" in *Gender, Families, and Elder Care,* eds. Jeffrey Dwyer and Raymond T. Coward (Newbury Park, CA: Sage Publications, 1992), 120-131.

[73]Montgomery and Kamo, "Parent Care by Sons and Daughters," 220.

[74]Horowitz, "Methodological Issues in the Study of Gender within Family Caregiving Relationships," 132-150; Rosenthal and Martin-Matthews, "Families as Care-Providers versus Care-Managers?" 132-150.

[75]Eleanor Palo Stoller, "Parental Caregiving by Adult Children," *Journal of Marriage and the Family* 45(1983), 854.

[76]Francesca Cancian, *Love in America: Gender and Self Development* (New York: Cambridge University Press, 1987) makes this point about romantic love.

[77]For an example of a statistical analysis of data that distinguishes between the approaches of sons and daughters see Merril Silverstein, Tonya M. Parrott, and Vern L. Bengtson, "Factors That Predispose Middle-Aged Sons and Daughters to Provide Social Support to Older Parents," *Journal of Marriage and the Family* 57(1995):465-475.

[78]The first part of this chapter synthesizes findings reported in three journal articles, analyzing data provided by the pairs of sisters (Sarah H. Matthews and Tena Tarler Rosner, "Shared Filial Responsibility: The Family as the Primary Caregiver," *Journal of Marriage and the Family*, 50[1988]: 185-195); the sister-brother pairs (Sarah H. Matthews, "The Division of Filial Responsibility in Lone-Sister Sibling Groups," *Journal of Gerontology: Social Sciences*, 50B[1995]: S312-S320); and the brother pairs (Sarah H. Matthews and Jenifer Heidorn, "Meeting Filial Responsibilities in Brothers-Only Sibling Groups," *Journal of Gerontology: Social Sciences* 53B[1998]:S278-S286).

[79]Anthony McMahon, *Taking Care of Men: Sexual Politics in the Public Mind*. (New York: Cambridge University Press, 1999); Eleanor Palo Stoller, "Theoretical Perspectives on Caregiving Men," in *Men as Caregivers: Theory, Research, and Service Implications*, eds. Betty J. Kramer and Edward H. Thompson, Jr. (New York: Springer, 2002), 51-68.

[80]Karen D. Pyke and Vern L. Bengtson, "Caring More or Less: Individualistic and Collectivist Systems of Family Eldercare," *Journal of Marriage and the Family* 58(1996): 379-392.

[81]Matthews and Rosner, "Shared Filial Responsibility," 185-195.

[82]The argument presented here draws on Sarah H. Matthews, "Brothers and Parent Care: An Explanation for Sons' Under-representation," in *Men as Caregivers*, eds. Betty J. Kramer and Edward H. Thompson, Jr. (New York: Springer, 2002), 234-249

[83]Gary R. Lee, "Gender Differences in Family Caregiving," 120-131.

[84]Raymond T. Coward and Jeffrey W. Dwyer, "The Association of Gender, Sibling Network Composition, and Patterns of Parent Care by Adult Children," *Research on Aging* 12(1990):158-181; Glenna Spitze and John Logan, "Sons, Daughters, and Intergenerational Social Support," *Journal of Marriage and the Family* 52(1990):420-430; Connnidis, Rosenthal, and McMullin, "The Impact of Family Composition on Providing Help to Older Parents," 402-419. Martin-Matthews and Campbell, "Gender Roles, Employment and Informal Care," 129-143, report that brothers with sisters were significantly *less* likely to provide personal care if they had sisters but no brothers. The focus on "personal care," rather than a more global measure of care, may account for this difference.

[85]Coward and Dwyer, "The Association of Gender, Sibling Network Composition, and Patterns of Parent Care," 158-181; Merrill, *Caring for Elderly Parents*, 56-57; A. C. Mui, "Caring for Frail Elderly Parents: A Comparison of Adult Sons and Daughters," *The Gerontologist* 35(1995):86-93.

[86]Edward H. Thompson, Jr., "What's Unique about Men's Caregiving?" in *Men as Caregivers*, eds. Betty J. Kramer and Edward H. Thompson, Jr. (New York: Springer, 2002), 20-47.

[87]Lori D. Campbell and Anne Martin-Matthews, "Caring Sons: Exploring Men's Involvement in Filial Care," 57-79; Naomi Gerstel and Sally K. Gallagher, "Men's Caregiving: Gender and the Contingent Character of Care," *Gender and Society* 15(2001):197-217.

[88]Nancy J. Finley, "Theories of Family Labor as Applied to Gender Differences in Caregiving for Elderly Parents," *Journal of Marriage and the Family* 51(1989):79-86.

[89]Logan and Spitze, *Family Ties;* Rossi and Rossi, *Of Human Bonding.*

[90]Montgomery and Kamo, "Parent Care by Sons and Daughters," 213-230.

[91]See Matthews, "The Division of Filial Responsibility in Lone-Sister Sibling Groups," S312-S320; Matthews and Heidorn, "Meeting Filial Responsibilities in Brothers-Only Siblings Groups," S278-S286. This tendency means that brothers, and men more generally, underreport their contributions to their parents, thus making men's and women's data difficult to compare.

[92]Merrill, "*Caring for Elderly Parents,*" 55, for example, quotes a sister who complained about her brother: "My brother comes on Friday night to cook their dinner and then again on Sunday to spend the day. But he says that he can't do more *to help me*" (emphasis added).

[93]Marshall, Matthews, and Rosenthal, "Elusiveness of Family Life." 39-72; Allen, Blieszner, and Roberto, "Families in the Middle and Later Years," 911-926.

[94]Logan and Sptize, *Family Ties,* make a different but related point: parents continue to provide more services and support to their children than they receive, unless they become incapacitated — a fate many parents escape.

[95]Recall from Chapter 2 the sister who provided round-the-clock care to her bedridden mother, describing how her very early day began: "I dress myself. She gets upset if I go into her room with my nightgown on. I think she wants to see me in my work clothes."

[96]In a growing number of studies, the perspectives of parents or parents and children, typically a mother and a daughter, are included. Most of these studies focus on how parents' feel about being the recipients of care. See, for example, Jane Aronson, "Old Women's Experiences of Needing Care: Choice or Compulsion?" *Canadian Journal on Aging* 9(1990): 234-247; Laura M. Donorfio and Nancy W. Sheehan, "Relationship Dynamics between Aging Mothers and Caregiving Daughters: Filial Expectations and Responsibilities," *Journal of Adult Development* 8(2001):39-49; Susan A. Eisenhandler, "Lifelong Roles and Cameo Appearances: Elderly Parents and Relationships with Adult Children," *Journal of Aging Studies* 6(1992):243-257; Nancy W. Sheehan and Laura M. Donorfio, "Efforts to Create Meaning in the Relationship between Aging Mothers and their Caregiving Daughters: A Qualitative Study of Caregiving," *Journal of Aging Studies* 13(1999):161-176; Maria M Talbott, "The Negative Side of the Relationship between Older Widows and their Adult Children: The Mother's Perspective," *The Gerontologist* 30(1990):595-603.

[97]In earlier work [Sarah H. Matthews, *The Social World of Old Women: Management of Self Identity* (Beverly Hills, CA: Sage, 1979), 123], I argued that old widowed mothers are dependent on their adult children: "The importance of maintaining the relationship is great, and explains the necessity of complying with the definition of her position

in the family as handed down by her offspring." This suggests that parents consider the potential consequences of not complying with their children's expectations. Research on older family ties that included siblings' parents could speak to this apparent contradiction.

[98]But see Judith C. Barker, "Neighbors, Friends, and Other Nonkin Caregivers of Community-Living Dependent Elders," *Journal of Gerontology: Social Sciences* 57B(2002): S158-S167; Hazel McRae, "Fictive Kin as a Component of the Social Networks of Older People," *Research on Aging* 14(1992):226-247; Eleanor Palo Stoller and Karen L. Pugliesi, "Informal Networks of Community-Based Elderly: Changes in Composition over Time," *Research on Aging* 10(1988): 499-516; Stoller and Pugliesi, "Size and Effectiveness of Informal Helping Networks: A Panel Study of Older People in the Community," *Journal of Health and Social Behavior* 32(1991):180-191.

[99]Shirley L. O'Bryant, "Neighbors' Support of Older Widows Who Live Alone in their Own Homes," *The Gerontologist* 25(1985):305-310.

[100]Shirley L. O'Bryant, "Sibling Support and Older Widow's Well-being," *Journal of Marriage and the Family* 50(1988): 173-183. For a review of the more general research literature on adult siblings, see Ingrid Connidis, *Family Ties and Aging* (Thousand Oaks, CA: Sage Publications, 2001), Chapter 12.

[101]Lori D. Campbell, Ingrid Arnet Connidis, and Lorraine Davies. "Sibling Ties in Later Life: A Social Network Analysis," *Journal of Family Issues* 20(1999):114-148; Ingrid Arnet Connidis, "Siblings as Friends in Later Life," *American*

Behavioral Scientist 33(1989):81-93; Connidis, "Sibling Support in Older Age," *Journal of Gerontology: Social Sciences* 49(1994b):S309-S319; Deborah T. Gold, "Siblings in Old Age: Something Special," *Canadian Journal on Aging* 6(1987):199-215; Sonia Miner and Peter Uhlenberg, "Intragenerational Proximity and the Social Role of Sibling Neighbors after Midlife," *Family Relations* 46(1997):145-153.

[102]Deborah Merrill, *Caring for Elderly Parents.*

[103]Judith Globerman, "The Unencumbered Child: Family Reputation and Responsibilities in the Care of Relatives with Alzheimer's Disease," *Family Process* 34(1996):87-99.

[104]Hochschild, *Second Shift*, reports that husbands who have a traditional view of marriage assist their employed wives more than husbands who hold non-traditional views.

[105]Reading this, one wonders whether seven months is correct. This underlines the utility of tape-recorded interviews, although people routinely misspeak in conversations. More to the point, what is missing here is the view of the third sister. She seems to feel that her actions are justified; and if her version were available, the dynamics would be clearer.

[106]According to the respondent, neither of the proximate sisters was the favorite child.

[107]Ingrid Arnet Connidis, "Growing Up and Old Together: Some Observations on Families in Later Life," in *Aging: Canadian Perspectives*, eds. Victor Marshall and Barry McPherson (Peterborough, Ontario: Broadview, 1994a), 195-205.

[108]Elaine M Brody, Christine J. Hoffman, Morton H. Kleban, and Claire B. Schoonover, "Caregiving Daughters and their Local Siblings: Perceptions, Strains, and Interactions," *The Gerontologist* 29(1989):529-538; Victor G. Cicirelli, "Marital Disruption and Adult Children's Perceptions of their Siblings' Help to Elderly Parents," *Journal of Family Relations* 33(1984):613-621; Deborah J. Merrill, "Conflict and Cooperation among Adult Siblings During the Transition to the Role of Filial Caregiver," *Journal of Social and Personal Relationships* 13(1996):399-413.

[109]Lyn H. Lofland, "Loss and Human Connection: An Exploration into the Nature of the Social Bond," in *Personality, Roles, and Social Behavior,* eds. William Ickes and Eric S. Knowles (New York: Springer-Verlag, 1982), 23, writes, "Persons are connected to one another through the parts they play in one another's futures. To 'lose' certain persons is to lose certain futures, certain quite realistic possibilities for action."

[110]Sarah H. Matthews, "Perceptions of Fairness in the Division of Responsibility for Old Parents" *Social Justice Research* 1 (1987):425-437. See also Lerner et al., "Adult Children as Caregivers," 746-755.

[111]The probable bias introduced by recruiting pairs of siblings is evident here. Siblings who had irreparable relationships would not have volunteered for the study. In groups of three or more siblings there were members who were described in disparaging terms by respondents, as is evident in data presented in this and previous chapters. Respondent siblings criticizing one another was relatively rare. A random sample of dyadic sibling groups would very likely produce

a higher percentage whose future relationship was viewed as unimportant.

[112]Carolyn J. Rosenthal and Victor W. Marshall, "Head of the Family: Social Meaning and Structural Variability," *Canadian Journal of Sociology* 11(1986):183-198.

[113]Marshall, Matthews, and Rosenthal, "Elusiveness of Family Life: A Challenge for the Sociology of Aging," 39-72; see also Martin-Matthews, "Intergenerational Caregiving," 64-79.

[114]It is not unusual to identify as primary caregivers those whose parents claim that they need or receive help with only one or two tasks on a list of fifteen, thereby defining both someone who requires help with housework and someone who needs help with toileting as care recipients. Betty J. Kramer, "Gain in the Caregiving Experience: Where are We? What Next?" *The Gerontologist* 37(1997), 219, found 29 studies of caregiving that met the criterion "providing assistance in one or more activities of daily living (ADL) or instrumental activities of daily living (IADL)." For a less extreme but equally problematic example see Coward and Dwyer, "The Association of Gender, Sibling Network Composition, and Patterns of Parent Care by Adult Children," 158-181, who explored the effects of "sibling network" in a sample 683 adult-child caregivers who had been identified as providing informal care by an elderly parent in the 1982 National Long Term Care Survey. Informal caregivers were identified as those whose parents reported receiving help with at least one ADL task (bathing, dressing, toileting, getting in/out of bed, getting around inside, eating, continence) in the previous three months.

[115] See Logan and Spitze, *Family Ties,* for a similar conclusion based on a representative sample of a population.

[116] Kramer, "Gain in the Caregiving Experience," 218-232; Kathleen W. Piercy, "Theorizing about Family Caregiving: The Role of Responsibility," *Journal of Marriage and the Family* 60(1998),109-118; Walker, Martin, and Jones, "The Benefits and Costs of Caregiving and Care Receiving for Daughters and Mothers," S130-S139.

[117] John Mogey, "Families: Intergenerational and Generational Connections," 52.

[118] Dennis P. Hogan, David J. Eggebeen, and Sean M. Snaith, "The Well-being of Aging Americans with Very Old Parents," in *Aging and Generational Relations over the Life Course,* ed. Tamara Hareven (New York: Walter de Gruyter, 1996), 333.

[119] *ibid.*

[120] Diane N. Lye, "Adult Child-Parent Relationships," *Annual Review of Sociology* 22(1996):79-102.

[121] Alexis Walker, "Conceptual Perspectives on Gender and Family Caregiving," in *Gender, Families, and Elder Care,* eds. Jeffrey W. Dwyer and Raymond T. Coward (Newbury Park, CA: Sage Publications, 1992), 34-46. Similarly, Spitze and Logan, "Sons, Daughters, and Intergenerational Social Support," 428, conclude, "In the future, when one- and particularly two-child families are the norm, parents' relations with sons and daughters-in-law may come to resemble more closely those they have today with adult daughters." See also Rhonda J. V. Montgomery, "Gender Differences

in Patterns of Child-Parent Caregiving Relationships" 82, who asserts that "sons are unlikely to alter their parent-care activities. . . women must seek a way out of their tasks other than through sharing those tasks with men." The authors assume that the approach of daughters to parent care is better than that of sons. Implicitly, they argue that to make *genuine* contributions, sons would need to do what daughters do.

[122]Recent research has challenged the assertion by pointing to male caregivers who provide extraordinary care. See, for example, Lenard W. Kaye and Jeffrey S. Applegate, *Men as Caregivers to the Elderly.* (Boston: Lexington, 1990); Kaye and Applegate, "Older Men and the Family Caregiving Orientation," in *Older Men's Lives,* ed. Edward H. Thompson (Thousand Oaks, CA: Sage Publications, 1994), 218-236; Phyllis Braudy Harris, "Listening to Caregiving Sons: Misunderstood Realties," *The Gerontologist* 38(1998):342-352; Phyllis Braudy Harris and Joyce Bichler, *Men Giving Care: Reflections of Husbands and Sons* (New York: Garland, 1997); Phyllis Braudy Harris, "The Misunderstood Caregiver? A Qualitative Study of the Male Caregiver of Alzheimer's Disease Victims," *The Gerontologist,* 33(1993): 551-556. There is a difference, however, between the assertion that some men provide care and the assertion that men do their fair share.

[123]Deborah Tannen, *You Just Don't Understand: Men and Women in Conversation* (New York: Ballantine, 1990).

[124]Kurt Luescher and Karl Pillemer, "Intergenerational Ambivalence: A New Framework for the Study of Parent-Child Relations in Later Life," *Journal of Marriage and the Family* 60 (1998):413-425.

¹²⁵Jetse Sprey, "Time Bound," in *Minding the Time in Family Experience: Emerging Perspectives and Issues*, ed. Kerry J. Daly (New York: JAI, 2001), 50.

¹²⁶The use of the word "civilized" borrows from Barbara Ehrenreich (*Nickel and Dimed*, New York: Metropolitan Books, 2001), 214, whose concern is prompted by the plight of the poor: "Most civilized nations compensate for the inadequacy of wages by providing relatively generous public services such as health insurance, free or subsidized child care, subsidized housing, and effective public transportation. But the United States, for all its wealth, leaves its citizens to fend for themselves. . . ."

Appendix I.

Interview Guide

INTRODUCTION: You were asked to participate in this research because of the age of your parent(s). We are interested in finding out how the needs of old parents affect their adult offspring, that is, you and your sibling(s).

You have already filled out the questionnaire about your family. In order for me to ask you further questions, I need to get some idea of who is in your family and what your particular situation is like. (INTERVIEWER: Use page in questionnaire on which brothers and sisters are listed. Find out where each of them and the parent(s) live. Discuss them enough to become comfortable with their names.)

1. We chose the age of 75 as the minimum age for parents in our study because we felt that after that age people are likely to be dealing with some of the problems that accompany aging. What about your parents? Would you tell what (his, her, their) situation is like?
     PROBE: Where does (she, he, they) live?
        (Are, Is) (they, she, he) having any particular problems at the present time?
        (Have, Has) (they, she, he) had any particular problems in the past?
        Why do you think (they, he, she) (have, has) been able to avoid problems?

2. Have you discussed these (potential) problems with (either of) your parents?

3. Have you discussed these (potential) problems with any of your siblings?
   PROBE: Which siblings? Which problems?

4. Has your concern about your parent(s) affected your relationship with any of your siblings?
   PROBE: (For each sib) Increased contact, change in quality of relationship?

5. Is the way that you and your siblings work together similar to or different from the way you worked together when you were younger?
   PROBE: Could you give me an example of the way you worked together then and compare it to the current situation?

6. When it comes to providing for your parent(s), how do you and your sibling(s) divide the responsibilities?
   PROBE: Is there one of you whom your parent(s) would call if a problem arose?
   Is there someone who is available for daytime visits or emergencies, another for evening visits and emergencies?
   Does someone organize every one else's contributions?
   Can you give me specific examples of the types of things that each of you does?
   GOAL: What are considered responsibilities and who does them?

7. Why do you think that you have divided tasks in this
way?
    PROBE: Why does one person do one thing, an-
    other person, another thing?

8. Do you think that too much burden falls to you or one
of your siblings?
    PROBE: Do you think one of your siblings is not
    doing his/her fair share?
        Do you feel that you are doing too much or too
        little or that someone else is?
        Do you think that the way you and your sibling(s)
        have divided tasks is fair?

8a. How different do you think things would be if you had
(a, another) sister to share the responsibility for your
parent(s)? [Note that respondents were asked this question only in lone-sister and brothers-only families.]

9. How does your (holding a job, not holding a job) affect
the kinds of things you do for your parent(s)?

10. What about your sibling(s)? Do you think that whether
(she, he, they) (is, are) employed makes a difference in the
kinds of things (she, he, they) do for your parent(s)?

11. How has having (an) old parent(s) affected your plans in
recent years?
    PROBE: Does it affect your taking vacations, decisions
    about moving, decisions about getting or keeping a
    job, participation in community events?

12. What effect (did, do you think) your (mother's, father's) death (have, will have) on your relationship with your (surviving parent)?

    NOTE: If both parents are living, ask question once for each parent.

13. What effect will your (surviving parent's, parents') death(s) have on your relationships with each of your siblings?

14. I am going to give your examples of emergency situations in which your parents may have been or might become involved. For each, would you tell me what did or probably would happen and who would be most likely to be available to help?

    NOTE: If old parent lives with someone, find out who else might be available in case that person was away.

    a. If your parent fell and was unable to get to a telephone.

    b. If your parent was ill enough to stay in bed but not ill enough to require hospitalization *for a short period of time* (a week or so)?

    c. If your parent was ill enough to stay in bed but not ill enough to require hospitalization *for an indefinite period of time.*

    d. If your parent locked (himself, herself) out of the house?

    e. If your (mother, father, parents) were turned out of (her, his, their) current residence for some reason?

    f. If your (mother's, father's, parent's) living expenses were to increase dramatically?

g. IF APPLICABLE: If one of your parents were to die? If it were your mother? If it were your father?

h. If a physician recommended that your (mother, father) go to a nursing home for a *short-term stay*?

i. If a physician recommended that your (mother, father) go to a nursing home for an *indefinite stay*?

15. Now I am going to read a list of some kinds of help family members sometimes give to one another. During the past year what kinds of help did you and (each of) your sibling(s) give to your (mother, father, parents)? CIRCLE YES OR NO FOR EACH SIBLING. IF MORE THAN ONE SIBLING PROVIDED SAME KIND OF HELP, ASK: Which provided the most? [Note: accompanying grid is not included.]

a. provided a home

b. helped with childcare [not asked here, see below]

c. helped with job, occupation

d. gave financial help

e. gave advice

f. provided personal services, for example, errands

g. helped with household chores

h. helped with home repairs

i. provided personal care in illness

j. gave emotional or moral support

k. helped deal with agencies or organizations

l. gave some other kind of help not mentioned.

Is there some kind of help that you or your sibling(s) gave to your parent(s) which we did not include in this list? WHAT AND WHICH SIBLING?

16. Now I am going to read a similar list and I would like to know what kinds of help your (mother, father, parents) gave you and each of your siblings during the past year. Circle yes or no. If parent gave same kind of help to more than on adult child, ask: To which did (she, he, they) provided the most? (Put ranking in parentheses).
    a. provided a home
    b. helped with childcare
    c. helped with job, occupation
    d. gave financial help
    e. gave advice
    f. provided personal services, for example, errands
    g. helped with household chores
    h. helped with home repairs
    i. provided personal care in illness
    j. gave emotional or moral support
    k. helped deal with agencies or organizations
    l. gave some other kind of help not mentioned.

Is there some kind of help which (she, he, they) gave to you or your sibling(s) which we have not included in this list? WHAT AND TO WHOM?

17. You and your siblings are not the only people who may provide emotional and financial help or provide services to your parent(s). I am going to read a list of possible others and I would like you to tell me whether there is anyone in that category who does something for your parent(s) and what it is that each does.

a. Siblings-in-law (Ask specifically about each of R's siblings' spouses as well as R's spouse.
b. Grandchildren (Ask specifically about *each set* of R's sibling's children as well as his or her own).
c. Old parents' siblings (How many are still living? Does the old parent have any contact with them?)
d. Old parent's siblings-in-law (How many are still living? Does the old parent have any contact with them?)
e. Neighbors (Are there people in the neighborhood with whom the old parent(s) exchange(s) services?)
f. Friends (Does the old parent(s) have friends with whom (she, he) exchanges services?)
g. Church members or members of other organizations?
h. Social services, e.g., meals-on-wheels, transportation services, priests, public health nurse (free or subsidized)
i. Paid helpers, e.g., housekeeper, nurse's aide

Bibliography

Abel, Emily. *Who Cares for the Elderly? Public Policy and the Experiences of Adult Daughters.* Philadelphia: Temple University Press, 1991.

Allen, Graham A. *A Sociology of Friendship and Kinship.* Sydney, Australia: Allen and Unwin, 1979.

Allen, Katherine R., Rosemary Blieszner, and Karen A. Roberto. "Families in the Middle and Later Years: A Review and Critique of Research in the 1990s." *Journal of Marriage and the Family* 62(2000):911-926.

Arber, Sara and Jay Ginn. "The Meaning of Informal Care: Gender and the Contribution of Elderly People." *Ageing and Society* 10(1990):429-454.

--------."Gender Differences in Informal Care," *Health and Social Care in the Community* 3(1995):19-31.

--------."Gender Differences in the Relationship between Paid Employment and Informal Care." *Work, Employment and Society* 9(1995):445-471.

Aronson, Jane. "Old Women's Experiences of Needing Care: Choice or Compulsion?" *Canadian Journal on Aging* 9(1990):234-247.

Barer, Barbara M. and Colleen Leahy Johnson. "A Critique of the Caregiving Literature." *The Gerontologist* 30(1990):726-733.

Barker, Judith C. "Neighbors, Friends, and Other Nonkin Caregivers of Community-Living Dependent Elders." *Journal of Gerontology: Social Sciences* 57B(2002):S158-S167.

Bengtson, Vern L. and Sandi S. Schrader. "Parent-Child Relations." In *Research Instruments in Social Gerontology*, edited by David J. Mangen and Warren A. Peterson, 115-128. Vol. 2. Minneapolis: University of Minnesota Press, 1982.

Berman, Harry J. "The Validity of Role Reversal: A Hermeneutic Perspective." *Journal of Gerontological Social Work* 20(1993): 101-111.

Bernard, Jessie. *The Future of Marriage.* New York: World Publishing, 1972.

Briar, Katherine H. and Caren Kaplan. *The Family Caregiving Crisis.* Silver Spring, MD: National Association of Social Workers, 1990.

Brody, Elaine M. *Women in the Middle: Their Parent-Care Years.* New York: Springer, 1990.

Brody, Elaine M., Christine J. Hoffman, Morton H. Kleban, and Claire. B. Schoonover. "Caregiving Daughters and their Local Siblings: Perceptions, Strains, and Interactions." *The Gerontologist* 29(1989):529-538.

Cager, Constance T. "The Role of Valued Outcomes, Justifications, and Comparison Referents in Perceptions of Fairness among Dual-Earner Couples." *Journal of Family Issues* 19(1998):622-648.

Campbell, Lori D., Ingrid Arnet Connidis, and Lorraine Davies. "Sibling Ties in Later Life: A Social Network Analysis." *Journal of Family Issues* 20(1999):114-148.

Campbell, Lori D. and Anne Martin-Matthews. "Caring Sons: Exploring Men's Involvement in Filial Care." *Canadian Journal on Aging* 19(2000):57-79.

--------. "Primary and Proximate: The Importance of Coresidence and Being Primary Provider of Care for Men's Filial Care Involvement." *Journal of Family Issues* 21(2000):1006-1030.

Cancian, Francesca. *Love in America: Gender and Self Development.* New York: Cambridge University Press, 1987.

Cancian, Francesca and Stacey J. Oliker. *Caring and Gender.* Thousand Oaks, CA: Pine Forge Press, 2000.

Cicirelli, Victor G., "Marital Disruption and Adult Children's Perceptions of their Sibling's Help to Elderly Parents." *Journal of Family Relations* 33(1984):613-621.

Climo, Jacob. *Distant Parents.* New Brunswick, NJ: Rutgers University Press, 1992.

Coltrane, Scott. "Research on Household Labor: Modeling and Measuring the Social Embeddedness of Routine Family Work." *Journal of Marriage and the Family* 62(2000):1208-1233

Connidis, Ingrid Arnet. "Siblings as Friends in Later Life." *American Behavioral Scientist* 33(1989):81-93.

--------. "Life Transitions and the Adult Sibling Tie: A Qualitative Study." *Journal of Marriage and the Family* 54(1992):972-982.

--------. "Growing Up and Old Together: Some Observations on Families in Later Life." In *Aging: Canadian Perspectives*, edited by Victor Marshall and Barry McPherson, 195-205. Peterborough, Ontario: Broadview, 1994a.

--------. "Sibling Support in Older Age." *Journal of Gerontology: Social Sciences* 49(1994b):S309-S317.

--------. *Family Ties and Aging.* Thousand Oaks, CA: Sage Publications, 2001.

Connidis, Ingrid Arnet and Lori D. Campbell. "Closeness, Confiding, and Contact among Siblings in Middle and Late Adulthood." *Journal of Family Issues* 16(1995):722-745.

Connidis, Ingrid Arnet and Lorraine Davies. "Confidants and Companions: Choices in Later Life." *Journal of Gerontology: Social Sciences* 47(1992):S115-S122.

--------. "Confidants and Companions in Later Life: The Place of Family and Friends." *Journal of Gerontology: Social Sciences* 47(1992): S141-S149.

Connidis, Ingrid Arnet and Julie McMullin. "Social Support in Older Age: Assessing the Impact of Marital and Parent Status." *Canadian Journal on Aging* 13(1994):510-527.

Connidis, Ingrid Arnet, Carolyn J. Rosenthal, and Julie McMullin. "The Impact of Family Composition on Providing Help to Older Parents: A Study of Employed Adults." *Research on Aging* 18(1996):402-419.

Cowan, Ruth Schwartz. *More Work for Mother.* New York: Basic Books, 1983.

Coward, Raymond T. and Jeffrey W. Dwyer. "The Association of Gender, Sibling Network Composition, and Patterns of Parent Care by Adult Children." *Research on Aging* 12(1990):158-181.

Dautzenbert, Maaike. *Daughters Caring for Elderly Parents.* Maastricht, The Netherlands: Universitaire Pers Maastricht, 2000.

Devault, Marjorie L. *Feeding the Family: The Social Organization of "Caring" as Gendered Work.* Chicago: University of Chicago Press, 1991.

di Leonardo, Micaela. "The Female World of Cards and Holidays: Women, Families, and the Work of Kinship." In *Rethinking the Family: Some Feminist Questions*, edited by Barrie Thorne and Marilyn Yolom, 246-261. Boston: Northeastern University Press, 1992.

Donorfio, Laura M. and Nancy W. Sheehan. "Relationship Dynamics between Aging Mothers and Caregiving Daughters: Filial Expectations and Responsibilities." *Journal of Adult Development* 8(2001):39-49.

Ehrenreich, Barbara. *Nickel and Dimed.* New York: Metropolitan Books, 2001.

Eisenhandler, Susan A. "Lifelong Roles and Cameo Appearances: Elderly Parents and Relationships with Adult Children." *Journal of Aging Studies* 6(1992):243-257.

Elias, Norbert. *What is Sociology?* New York: Columbia University Press, 1978.

Farber, Bernard. *Family and Kinship in Modern Society.* Glenview, IL: Scott, Foresman, 1973.

Farrell, Betty. *Family: The Making of an Idea, an Institution, and a Controversy in American Culture.* Boulder, CO: Westview, 1999.

Finch, Janet. *Family Obligations and Social Change.* Cambridge, MA: Polity Press, 1989.

Finch, Janet and Jennifer Mason. "Filial Obligations and Kin Support for Elderly People." *Ageing and Society* 10(1990):151-175.

--------. "Obligations of Kinship in Contemporary Britain: Is There Normative Agreement?" *British Journal of Sociology* 42(1991): 345-367.

--------. *Negotiating Family Responsibilities.* New York: Tavistock/ Routledge, 1993.

Finley, Nancy J. "Theories of Family Labor as Applied to Gender Differences in Caregiving for Elderly Parents." *Journal of Marriage and the Family* 51(1989):79-86.

Franzen, Jonathan. *The Corrections.* New York: Farrar, Straus and Giroux, 2001.

Gee, Ellen M. and Gloria M. Gutman. *The Overselling of Population Aging: Apocalyptic Demography, Intergenerational Challenges, and Social Policy.* Don Mills, Ontario, Canada: Oxford University Press, 2000.

Gerstel, Naomi and Sally K. Gallagher. "Men's Caregiving: Gender and the Contingent Character of Care." *Gender and Society* 15(2001):197-217.

Globerman, Judith. "Motivations to Care: Daughters and Sons-in-law Caring for Relatives with Alzheimer's Disease." *Family Relations* 45(1996):37-45.

--------. "The Unencumbered Child: Family Reputation and Responsibilities in the Care of Relatives with Alzheimer's Disease." *Family Process* 34(1996):87-99.

Goetting, Ann. "Patterns of Support among In-laws in the United States." *Journal of Family Issues* 11(1990), 67-90.

Gold, Deborah T. "Siblings in Old Age: Something Special." *Canadian Journal on Aging* 6(1987):199-215.

Greenwell, Lisa and Vern L. Bengtson. "Geographic Distance and Contact between Middle-Aged Children and their Parents: The Effects of Social Class over 20 Years." *Journal of Gerontology: Social Sciences* 52B(1997):S13-S26.

Guberman, Nancy. "Daughters-in-law as Caregivers: How and Why Do They Come to Care?" *Journal of Women and Aging*: 11(1999): 85-102.

Hallman, Bonnie C. and Alun E. Joseph. "Getting There: Mapping the Gendered Geography of Caregiving to Elderly Relatives." *Canadian Journal on Aging* 18(1999):397-414.

Harris, Phyllis Braudy. "The Misunderstood Caregiver? A Qualitative Study of the Male Caregiver of Alzheimer's Disease Victims." *The Gerontologist* 33(1993): 551-556.

--------. "Listening to Caregiving Sons: Misunderstood Realties." *The Gerontologist* 38(1998):342-352.

Harris, Phyllis Braudy and Joyce Bichler. *Men Giving Care: Reflections of Husbands and Sons*. New York: Garland, 1997.

Hauser, Robert M., Jennifer T. Sheridan, and John Robert Warren. "Socioeconomic Achievements of Siblings in the Life Course: New Findings from the Wisconsin Longitudinal Study." *Research on Aging* 21(1999):338-378.

Himes, Christine L. "Parental Caregiving by Adult Women: A Demographic Perspective." *Research on Aging* 16(1994):191-211.

Hochschild, Arlie Russell with Anne Machung. *The Second Shift*. New York: Viking Penguin, 1989.

Hogan, Dennis P., David J. Eggebeen, and Sean M. Snaith. "The Well-being of Aging Americans with Very Old Parents." In *Aging and Generational Relations over the Life Course*, edited by Tamara Hareven, 327-346. New York: Walter de Gruyter, 1996.

Horowitz, Amy. "Sons and Daughters as Caregivers to Older Parents: Differences in Role Performance and Consequences." *The Gerontologist* 25(1985):612-617.

--------. "Methodological Issues in the Study of Gender within Family Caregiving Relationships." In *Gender, Families, and Elder Care*, edited by Jeffrey W. Dwyer and Raymond T. Coward, 132-150. Newbury Park, CA: Sage Publications, 1992.

Houser, Betsy Bosak, Sherry L. Berkman, and Phil Bardsley. "Sex and Birth Order Differences in Filial Behavior." *Sex Roles* 13(1985): 641-651.

Ikels, Charlotte. "The Process of Caretaker Selection." *Research on Aging* 5(1983):491-509.

Ingersoll-Dayton, Berit, Marjorie E. Starrels, and David Dowler. "Caregiving for Parents and Parents-in-law: Is Gender Important?" *The Gerontologist* 36(1996):483-491.

Johnson, Colleen Leahy. *Ex Familia: Grandparents, Parents and Children Adjust to Divorce.* New Brunswick, NJ: Rutgers University Press, 1988.

Joseph, Alun E. and Bonnie C. Hallman, "Caught in the Triangle: The Influence of Home, Work, and Elderly Location on Work-Family Balance." *Canadian Journal on Aging* 15(1996):393-412.

Kahn, Michael D. and Stephen Bank. "In Pursuit of Sisterhood: Adult Siblings as a Resource for Combined Individual and Family Therapy." *Family Process* 20(1981):85-95

Katz, Sidney, Amasa B. Ford, Roland W. Moskowitz, Beverly A. Jackson, and Marjorie W. Jaffe. "Studies of Illness in the Aged." *Journal of the American Medical Association*, 185(1963):914-919.

Kaye, Lenard W. and Jeffrey S. Applegate. *Men as Caregivers to the Elderly.* Boston: Lexington, 1990.

--------. "Older Men and the Family Caregiving Orientation." In *Older Men's Lives*, edited by Edward H. Thompson, 218-236. Thousand Oaks, CA: Sage Publications, 1994.

Keith, Carolyn. "Family Caregiving Systems: Models, Resources, and Values." *Journal of Marriage and the Family* 57(1995):179-189.

Kessler, Suzanne and Wendy McKenna. *Gender: An Ethnomethodological Approach.* New York: Wiley-Interscience, 1978.

Kingsmill, Suzanne and Benjamin Schlesinger. *The Family Squeeze: Surviving the Sandwich Generation.* Toronto: University of Toronto Press, 1998.

Kivett, Vira R. "Mother-in-law and Daughter-in-law Relations." In *Aging Parents and Adult Children*, edited by Jay Mancini, 18-32. Lexington, MA: Lexington Books, 1989.

Kleban Morton H., Elaine M. Brody, Claire B. Schoonover, and Christine Hoffman. "Family Help to the Elderly: Perceptions of Sons-in-law Regarding Parent care." *Journal of Marriage and the Family* 51(1989):303-312.

Kluwer, Esther S., Jose A. M. Heesink, and Evert Van De Vliert. "The Marital Dynamics of Conflict over the Division of Labor." *Journal of Marriage and the Family* 59(1997):635-653.

Kramer, Betty J. "Gain in the Caregiving Experience: Where are We? What Next?" *The Gerontologist* 37(1997):218-232.

Lee, Gary R. "Gender Differences in Family Caregiving: A Fact in Search of a Theory." In *Gender, Families, and Elder Care* edited by Jeffrey W. Dwyer and Raymond T. Coward, 120-131. Newbury Park, CA: Sage Publications, 1992.

Lee, Gary R., Jeffrey W. Dwyer, and Raymond T. Coward. (1993). "Gender Differences in Parent Care: Demographic Factors and Same-Gender Preferences." *Journal of Gerontology: Social Sciences* 48(1993):S9-S16.

Lee, Gary R., Julie K. Netzer, and Raymond T. Coward. "Filial Responsibility Expectations and Patterns of Intergenerational Assistance." *Journal of Marriage and the Family* 56(1994):559-565.

Lerner Melvin J., Darryl G. Somers, David Reid, David Chiriboga, and Mary Tierney. "Adult Children as Caregivers: Egocentric Biases in Judgments of Sibling Contributions." *The Gerontologist* 31(1991):746-755.

Litwak, Eugene. "Extended Kin Relations in an Industrial Democratic Society." In *Social Structure and the Family*, edited by Ethel Shanas and Gordon F. Streib, 290-323. Englewood Cliffs, NJ: Prentice-Hall, 1965.

--------. *Helping the elderly: The Complementary Roles of Informal Networks and Formal Systems.* New York: Guilford, 1985.

Lofland, John and Lyn H. Lofland. *Analyzing Social Settings.* Belmont, CA: Wadsworth, 1995.

Lofland, Lyn H. "Loss and Human Connection: An Exploration into the Nature of the Social Bond" in *Personality, Roles, and Social Behavior*, edited by William Ickes and Eric S. Knowles, 219-242. New York: Springer-Verlag, 1982.

Logan, John R. and Glenna D. Spitze. *Family Ties: Enduring Relations between Parents and their Grown Children.* Philadelphia: Temple University Press, 1996.

Looker, E. Dianne. "Images of Work: Women's Work, Men's Work, Housework." *Canadian Journal of Sociology* 27(1999):225-254.

Loomis, Laura Spencer and Alan Booth. "Multigenerational Caregiving and Well-being: The Myth of the Beleaguered Sandwich Generation." *Journal of Family Issues* 16(1995):131-148.

Luescher, Kurt and Karl Pillemer. "Intergenerational Ambivalence: A New Framework for the Study of Parent-Child Relations in Later Life." *Journal of Marriage and the Family* 60(1998):413-425.

Lye, Diane N. "Adult Child-Parent Relationships." *Annual Review of Sociology* 22(1996):79-102.

Macken, Candace L. "Profile of Functionally Impaired Elderly Persons Living in the Community." *Health Care Financing Review* 7(1986):33-49.

Mangen, David J., Vern L. Bengtson, and Pierre H. Landry, Jr. *Measurement of Intergenerational Relations.* Beverly Hills, CA: Sage Publications, 1988.

Marshall, Victor W., Sarah H. Matthews, and Carolyn J. Rosenthal. "Elusiveness of Family Life: A Challenge for the Sociology of Aging." *Annual Review of Gerontology and Geriatrics* 13(1993): 39-72.

Martin-Matthews, Anne. "Intergenerational Caregiving: How Apocalyptic and Dominant Demographies Frame the Questions and Shape the Answers." In *The Overselling of Population Aging: Apocalyptic Demography, Intergenerational Challenges, and Social Policy,* edited by Ellen M. Gee and Gloria M. Gutman, 64-79. Don Mills, Ontario, Canada: Oxford University Press, 2000.

Martin-Matthews, Anne and Lori D. Campbell. "Gender Roles, Employment and Informal Care." In *Connecting Gender And Ageing: A Sociological Approach* edited by Sara Arber and Jay Ginn, 129-143. Philadelphia, PA: Open University Press, 1995.

Martin-Matthews, Anne and Carolyn J. Rosenthal. "Balancing Work and the Family in an Aging Society." *Annual Review of Gerontology and Geriatrics* 13(1993):96-117.

Matthews, Sarah H. *The Social World of Old Women: Management of Self Identity.* Beverly Hills, CA: Sage Publications, 1979

--------. "Perceptions of Fairness in the Division of Responsibility for Old Parents." *Social Justice Research* 1(1987):425-437.

--------. "The Burdens of Parentcare." *Journal of Aging Studies* 2(1988): 158-165.

--------. "Men's Ties to Siblings in Old Age: Contributing Factors to Availability and Quality." In *Older Men's Lives* edited by Edward H. Thompson, Jr., 178-196. Thousand Oaks, CA: Sage Publications, 1994.

--------. "The Division of Filial Responsibility in Lone-Sister Sibling Groups." *Journal of Gerontology: Social Sciences* 50B(1995), S312-320.

--------. "Brothers and Parent Care: An Explanation for Sons' Underrepresentation." In *Men as Caregivers* edited by Betty J. Kramer and Edward H. Thompson, Jr., 234-249. New York: Springer, 2002.

Matthews, Sarah H., Margaret E. Adamek, and Ruth E. Dunkle. "Research on Older Families When More than One Member Responds." *Journal of Aging Studies* 7(1993):215-228.

Matthews, Sarah H., Paula J. Delaney, and Margaret E. Adamek. "Male Kinship Ties: Bonds between Adult Brothers." *American Behavioral Scien*tist 33(1989):58-69.

Matthews, Sarah H. and Jenifer Heidorn. "Meeting Filial Responsibilities in Brothers-Only Sibling Groups." *Journal of Gerontology: Social Sciences* 53B(1998):S278-S286.

Matthews, Sarah H. and Tena Tarler Rosner. "Shared Filial Responsibility: The Family as the Primary Caregiver." *Journal of Marriage and the Family* 50(1988):185-195.

Matthews, Sarah H. and Jetse Sprey. "The Perils of Drawing Policy Implications from Research: The Case of Elder Mistreatment." In *Elder Abuse: Practice and Policy*, edited by Rachel Filinson and Stanley R. Ingman, 51-61. New York: Human Sciences Press, 1989.

Matthews, Sarah H., Janet E. Werkner, and Paula J. Delaney. "Relative Contributions of Help by Employed and Nonemployed Sisters to their Elderly Parents." *Journal of Gerontology: Social Sciences* 44(1989):S36-S44.

McMahon, Anthony. *Taking Care of Men: Sexual Politics in the Public Mind*. New York: Cambridge University Press, 1999.

McRae, Hazel. "Fictive Kin as a Component of the Social Networks of Older People." *Research on Aging* 14(1992):226-247.

Merrill, Deborah J. "Daughters-in-law as Caregivers to the Elderly." *Research on Aging* 15(1993):70-91.

--------. "Conflict and Cooperation among Adult Siblings During the Transition to the Role of Filial Caregiver. *Journal of Social and Personal Relationships* 13(1996):399-413.

--------. *Caring for Elderly Parents: Juggling Work, Family, and Caregiving in Middle and Working Class Families*. Westport, CT: Auburn House, 1997.

Miner, Sonia and Peter Uhlenberg. "Intragenerational Proximity and the Social Role of Sibling Neighbors after Midlife." *Family Relations* 46(1997):145-153.

Mogey, John. "Families: Intergenerational and Generational Connections—Conceptual Approaches to Kinship and Culture." In *Families: Intergenerational and Generational Connections*, edited by Susan K. Pfeifer and Marvin B. Sussman, 47-67. New York: Haworth, 1991.

Montgomery, Rhonda J. V. "Gender Differences in Patterns of Child-Parent Caregiving Relationships." In *Gender, Families, and Elder Care*, edited by Jeffrey W. Dwyer and Raymond T. Coward, 65-83. Newbury Park, CA: Sage Publications, 1992.

--------. "The Family Role in the Context of Long-term Care." *Journal of Aging and Health* 11(1999):383-416.

Montgomery, R. J. V. and Y. Kamo. "Parent Care by Sons and Daughters." In *Aging Parents and Adult Children*, edited by Jay Mancini, 213-230. Lexington, MA: Lexington Books, 1989.

Mui, A. C. "Caring for Frail Elderly Parents: A Comparison of Adult Sons and Daughters." *The Gerontologist* 35(1995):86-93.

Neal, Margaret B., Berit Ingersoll-Dayton, and Marjorie E. Starrels. "Gender and Relationship Differences in Caregiving Patterns and Consequences among Employed Caregivers." *The Gerontologist* 37(1997):804-816.

Neugarten, Bernice L. "Age Groups in American Society and the Rise of the Young-Old." *Annals of the American Academy* 415(1974): 187-198.

Neugarten, Bernice L. and Dale A. Neugarten. "Aging in the Aging Society." *Daedalus* 115(1986):31-49.

O'Bryant, Shirley L. "Neighbors' Support of Older Widows Who Live Alone in their Own Homes." *The Gerontologist* 25(1985): 305-310.

--------. "Sibling Support and Older Widow's Well-Being." *Journal of Marriage and the Family* 50(1988):173-183.

Pampel, Fred. *Aging, Social Inequality, and Public Policy.* Thousand Oaks, CA: Pine Forge Press, 1998.

Parrott, Tonya M. and Vern L. Bengtson. "The Effects of Earlier Intergenerational Affection, Normative Expectations, and Conflict on Contemporary Exchanges of Help and Support." *Research on Aging* 21(1999):73-105.

Pavalko, Eliza K. and Julie E. Artis. "Women's Caregiving and Paid Work: Causal Relationships in Late Midlife." *Journal of Gerontology: Social Sciences* 52B(1997):S170-S179.

Peters-Davis, Nora D., Miriam S. Moss, and Rachel A. Pruchno. "Children-in-law in Caregiving Families." *The Gerontologist* 39(1999):66-75.

Piercy, Kathleen W. "Theorizing about Family Caregiving: The Role of Responsibility." *Journal of Marriage and the Family* 60(1998): 109-118.

Pyke, Karen D. and Vern L. Bengtson. "Caring More or Less: Individualistic and Collectivist Systems of Family Eldercare." *Journal of Marriage and the Family* 58(1996):379-392.

Reskin, Barbara and Irene Padavic. *Women and Men at Work.* Thousand Oaks, CA: Pine Forge Press, 1994.

Riley, Matilda White. "The Family in an Aging Society: A Matrix of Latent Relationships." *Journal of Family Issues* 4(1983):439-454.

Robison, Julie, Phyllis Moen, and Donna Dempster-McClain. "Women's Caregiving: Changing Profiles and Pathways." *Journal of Gerontology: Social Sciences* 50B(1995):S362-S373.

Rosenthal, Carolyn J. "Kinkeeping in the Familial Division of Labor." *Journal of Marriage and the Family* 47(1985):956-974.

Rosenthal, Carolyn J. and Victor W. Marshall. "Head of the Family: Social Meaning and Structural Variability." *Canadian Journal of Sociology* 11(1986):183-198.

Rosenthal, Carolyn J. and Anne Martin-Matthews. "Families as Care-Providers versus Care-Managers? Gender and Type of Care in a Sample of Employed Canadians." SEDAP Research Paper No. 4, Hamilton, Ontario Canada: McMaster University, 1999.

Rosenthal, Carolyn J., Anne Martin-Matthews, and Sarah H. Matthews. "Caught in the Middle? Occupancy in Multiple Roles and Help to Parents in a National Probability Sample of Canadian Adults." *Journal of Gerontology: Social Sciences* 51B(1996):S274-S283.

Rossi, Alice S. and Peter H. Rossi. *Of Human Bonding: Parent-Child Relations across the Life Course.* New York: Aldine de Gruyter, 1990.

Seidel, John V., Rolf Kjolseth, and Elaine Seymour. *The Ethnograph.* Littleton, CO: Qualis Research Associates, 1988.

Scharlach, Andrew E. "Caregiving and Employment: Competing or Complementary Roles?" *The Gerontologist* 34(1994):378-385.

Shanas, Ethel. *The Health of Older People: A Social Survey.* Cambridge, MA: Harvard University Press, 1962.

--------. "Social Myth as Hypothesis: The Case of the Family Relations of Old People." *The Gerontologist* 19(1979):3-9.

Shanas, Ethel, Peter Townsend, D. Wedderburn, H. Friis, P. Hilhof, and J. Stehouwer. *Old People in Three Industrial Societies.* New York: Atherton Press, 1968.

Shaw, Susan M. "Gender Differences in the Definition and Perception of Household Labor." *Family Relations* 37(1988):333-337.

Sheehan, Nancy W. and Laura M. Donorfio. "Efforts to Create Meaning in the Relationship between Aging Mothers and their Caregiving Daughters: A Qualitative Study of Caregiving." *Journal of Aging Studies* 13(1999):161-176.

Shelton, Beth Anne and Daphne John. "The Division of Household Labor." *Annual Review of Sociology* 22(1996):299-322.

Silverstein, Merril. "Stability and Change in Temporal Distance between the Elderly and their Children." *Demography* 32(1995):29-45.

Silverstein, Merril, Xuan Chen, and Kenneth Heller. "Too Much Of A Good Thing? Intergenerational Social Support and The Psychological Well-being of Older Parents." *Journal of Marriage and the Family* 58(1996):970-982.

Silverstein, Merril., Tonya M. Parrott, and Vern L. Bengtson. "Factors That Predispose Middle-Aged Sons and Daughters to Provide Social Support to Older Parents." *Journal of Marriage and the Family* 57(1995):465-475.

Spitze, Glenna and John Logan. "More Evidence On Women (and Men) in The Middle." *Research on Aging* 14(1990):291-312.

--------. "Sons, Daughters, and Intergenerational Social Support." *Journal of Marriage and the Family* 52(1990):420-430.

--------. "Employment and Filial Relations: Is There a Conflict?" *Sociological Forum* 6(1991):681-697.

--------. "Helping as a Component of Parent-Adult Child Relations." *Research on Aging* 14(1992):291-312.

Sprey, Jetse. "Time Bound." In *Minding the Time in Family Experience: Emerging Perspectives and Issues*, edited by Kerry J. Daly, 37-57. New York: JAI, 2001.

Stoller, Eleanor Palo. "Parental Caregiving by Adult Children." *Journal of Marriage and the Family* 45(1983):851-858.

--------. "Teaching about Gender: The Experience of Family Care of Frail Elderly Relatives." *Educational Gerontology* 20(1994):679-697.

--------. "Theoretical Perspectives on Caregiving Men." In *Men as Caregivers: Theory, Research, and Service Implications*, edited by Betty J. Kramer and Edward H. Thompson, Jr., 51-68. New York: Springer, 2002.

Stoller, Eleanor Palo, Loran Earl Forster, and Tamara Sutin Duniho. "Systems of Parent Care within Sibling Networks." *Research on Aging* 14(1992):28-49.

Stoller, Eleanor Palo and Karen L. Pugliesi. "Informal Networks of Community-Based Elderly: Change in Composition over Time." *Research on Aging* 10(1988):499-516.

--------. "Other Roles of Caregivers: Competing Responsibilities or Supportive Resources." *Journal of Gerontology: Social Sciences* 44(1989):S231-S238.

--------. "Size and Effectiveness of Informal Helping Networks: A Panel Study of Older People in the Community." *Journal of Health and Social Behavior* 32(1991):180-191.

Stone, Robyn, Gail L. Cafferata, and Judith Sangl. "Caregivers of the Frail Elderly: A National Profile." *The Gerontologist* 27(1987): 616-626.

Strawbridge, William L. and Margaret I. Wallhagen. "Impact of Family Conflict on Adult Caregivers." *The Gerontologist* 31(1991):770-777.

Stull, Donald E., Karen Bowman, and Virginia Smerglia. "Women in the Middle: A Myth in the Making?" *Family Relations* 43(1994): 319-324.

Talbott, Maria M. "The Negative Side of the Relationship between Older Widows and their Adult Children: The Mothers' Perspective." *The Gerontologist* 30(1990):595-603.

Tannen, Deborah. *You Just Don't Understand: Men and Women in Conversation*. New York: Ballantine, 1990.

Thompson, Edward H., Jr. "What's Unique about Men's Cargiving?" In *Men as Caregivers*, edited by Betty J. Kramer and Edward H. Thompson, Jr., 20-47. New York: Springer, 2002.

Townsend, Peter. "The Structured Dependency of the Elderly." *Ageing and Society* 1(1981):5-28.

Ungerson, Clare. "Women and Caring: Skills, Tasks and Taboos." In *The Public and the Private*, edited by Eva Gamarnikow, David H. J. Morgan, June Purvis, and Daphne Taylorson, 62-77. London: Heinemann, 1983.

Walker, Alexis J. "Conceptual Perspectives on Gender and Family Caregiving." In *Gender, Families, and Elder Care* edited by Jeffrey W. Dwyer and Raymond T. Coward, 34-46. Newbury Park, CA: Sage Publications, 1992.

Walker, Alexis J., Sally S. K. Martin, and Laura L. Jones. "The Benefits and Costs of Caregiving and Care Receiving for Daughters and Mothers." *Journal of Gerontology: Social Sciences* 47(1992):S130-S139.

Walker, Alexis J. and Clara C. Pratt. *Sampling Bias in Family Caregiving Studies: A Research Note*. Paper presented at the Annual Meetings of the Gerontological Society of America, November, 1989.

--------. "Daughters' Help to Mothers: Intergenerational Aid versus Caregiving." *Journal of Marriage and the Family* 53(1991):3-12.

Walker, Alexis J., Clara C. Pratt, and Linda Eddy. "Informal Caregiving to Aging Family Members: A Critical Review." *Family Relations* 44(1995):402-411.

Weiss, Robert S. *Learning from Strangers: The Art and Method of Qualitative Interview Studies*. New York: Free Press, 1994.

White, Lynn K. "Sibling Relationships over the Life Course: A Panel Analysis." *Journal of Marriage and Family* 63(2001):555-568.

White, Lynn K. and Agnes Riedmann. "Ties among Adult Siblings." *Social Forces* 7(1992):85-102.

Wolf, Douglas A., Vicki Freedman, and Beth J. Soldo. "The Division of Family Labor: Care for Elderly Parents." *Journal of Gerontology: Social Sciences* 52B(1997, Special Issue):102-109.

Young, Michael and Peter Willmott. *Family and Class in a London Suburb*. London: Routledge and Kegan Paul, 1960.

Zimmerman, Rick S., David J. Jackson, Charles F. Longino, Jr., and Julia E. Bradsher. "Interpersonal and Economic Resources as Mediators of the Effects of Health Decline on the Geographic Mobility of the Elderly." *Journal of Aging and Health* 5(1993):37-57.

INDEX

McRae, Hazel 242
Merrill, Deborah J. 218, 229, 239, 240, 243-4
Miner, Sonia 243
Moen, Phyllis 235
Mogey, John 13, 211, 220, 246
Money issues 43-4, 54, 76-8, 83, 91, 101-2, 116, 117, 136, 178, 186, 189,
    191, 197, 199, 200, 211
Monitoring parents 124-6, 135, 138, 139, 143, 157, 163, 214-5
Montgomery, Rhonda J. V. 229, 236, 237, 240, 246
Moskowitz, Roland W. 222
Moss, Miriam S. 230
Mui, A. C. 239

Neal, Margaret B. 232, 236
Neighbors, parents 33, 51, 162, 164-9, 173
Netzer, Julie K. 218
Neugarten, Bernice L. 16, 221, 224
Neugarten, Dale A. 224

O'Bryant, Shirley L. 242
Obedient style 143, 152, 157, 177, 186, 215
Oliker, Stacey J. 232

Padavic, Irene 232
Pampel, Fred 228
Parents
    Brothers of 170-1
    Capable 33-7
    Couples 46-50
    Dependent 38-45
    Extended Kin of 133, 171
    In-between 46-61
    Personality 50-53
    Self-sufficient 55, 130, 131, 134, 135, 137, 144, 146, 180, 212, 215
    Sisters of 169-170
Parents as "burdens" 30-1, 146-7, 149, 151, 177, 178, 185, 200, 204,
    210-1, 234, 251

ABOUT THE AUTHOR

Sarah H. Matthews is Professor of Sociology at Cleveland State University. She is on the editorial boards of *Journal of Aging Studies, Journal of Marriage and Family,* and *The International Journal of Aging and Human Development.* She is the author of two previous books, *The Social World of Old Women: Management of Self-Identity* and *Friendships through the Life Course: Oral Biographies in Old Age,* and has published numerous articles about older family ties in gerontology journals and edited books.

Printed in the United States
6695